MAOIST INSURGENCY IN NEPAL
The Challenge and the Response

MAOIST INSURGENCY IN NEPAL
The Challenge and the Response

S.D. Muni

Rupa & Co

in association with
Observer Research Foundation

Contents

Acknowledgements

This study is the outcome of Mr M. Rasgotra's kind and affectionate persuasion. In the course of an in-house discussion on Nepal Centre's research programme, I suggested a few themes on which studies could be commissioned. "The Maoists Problem of Nepal" was one of those themes. Mr Rasgotra insisted that I must undertake this study and there was no way I could resist his command despite my numerous other preoccupations

I have been considerably benefited in preparing this study from the Observer Research Foundation's (ORF's) Nepal Bulletin prepared by Dr Sangeeta Thapliyal. This source supplemented the web sources and limited access to the Nepalese dialogues organized by the ORF have also been of immense utility in discussing some of my ideas and learning from my Nepalese friends. My three visits to Nepal in connection with other international conferences also gave me the much needed opportunity to interact with mainstream political parties' leaders as also a number of journalists and academics in the Kingdom. I was also fortunate in being able to discuss some of the sensitive questions with the high ranking Maoist leaders and senior officers in the Government of India dealing with Nepal policy. Brief meetings with the US and international organisations' officers passing through Delhi also provided valuable inputs. The insights and information provided in the course of these interactions have gone a long way in helping me understand the nuances and complexities of the Maoist insurgency.

In writing this book, I was expected not to exceed 10,000 words, but I could not help going much beyond that limit. I thought it may be better to put the available material at one place in an organised form. The length may be cumbersome for a reader but the spread of the information available may help serve diverse interests. Hope my friends will be generous in offering their constructive criticism on this book so as to point out its shortcomings and gaps.

New Delhi   S.D. Muni
April 21, 2003

I

The Roots and the Emergence
of the Maoists

The Maoist insurgency has emerged as one of the most serious political and security challenge in Nepal, with its disturbing implications for the adjoining regions in India. The rise of the insurgency is dated to February 1996. It has, by now, taken a toll of some 7500 lives with many more casualties. The numbers of these casualties and deaths have swelled rather significantly after November 2001 when an open confrontation, almost a civil war, broke out between the Royal Nepal Army (RNA) and the Maoists. After about fourteen months of this civil war, the Maoists and the Nepalese government, now led by the King with a puppet government, agreed on 29 January 2003, to agree to a ceasefire and start negotiations; thus going back to the situation that existed before the outbreak of the civil war. In this paper, we propose to look at the nature of the insurgency and the prospects of its solution.

The roots of the Maoists can be traced to the Communist movement in Nepal, which took birth in India in 1949 with the aim of actively participating in the anti-Rana struggle of 1950–51. When the first general elections of Nepal were held in 1959, under a Constitution to establish democracy with Constitutional Monarchy the communists were still very weak and isolated. They won barely four seats in the elections and did not count for much political influence. The Communists got split on the question of support to King Mahendra's takeover in December 1960, from the then elected government of the Nepali Congress, led by the charismatic leader B.P. Koirala, barely after it had been in office for 18 months. The faction of the Communist Party that sided with the palace got support and encouragement since the King wanted to use the Communists for countering the Nepali Congress and all other democratic forces opposing his direct rule, which was subsequently protected under the Panchayat System. The evolution of the Communist Movement in Nepal was also influenced by developments in the International Communist Movement, particularly the Sino-Soviet split, but it may be a digression to go into the details of those developments here. It is pertinent here to note that at least until the latter half of the 1960s, both the pro-Soviet and the pro-Chinese Communist factions operating within Nepal supported the King and his Panchayat System. The only exception was the Communist faction led by Pushpalal, who still operated from his base in India and worked along with the Nepali Congress to oppose the King and his system. The interests of the Nepal-based Communist groups converged on opposing the Nepali Congress led democratic resistance to the King, as that was seen to be receiving support and sustenance from India. The so-called anti-India nationalism was whipped up by King Mahendra and his associates and made a binding thread between the King and the divergent Communist factions.

Towards the latter half of the 1960s and early 1970s, the Communist Movement in Nepal also developed its extremist sections. Their rise was influenced by the Chinese cultural revolution and the rise of Maoists in India who came to be known as the Naxalites, because of the area of *Naxal Bari* in West Bengal where they started their early operations. Following the footsteps of the Indian Naxalites, the Nepali Communist Party (Marxist-Leninist) also carried out killings of the local feudals in the Jhapa area of eastern Nepal during the early 1970s. This is known in Nepal's contemporary history as the Jhapali uprising. Nirmal Lama and Mohan Bikram Singh led different Maoists factions of the Nepal Communist Parties between the early 1970s and the Peoples' Revolution (*Jan Andolan*) of 1989–90. The areas of their ideological and military operations were located mainly in the western and central-western hills as well as eastern Nepal. Around the 1980s, these extremist groups had been joined by young, well educated and ideologically motivated leaders like Dr Baburam Bhattarai and Pushpa Kamal Dahal-Prachanda.[1] The factional divisions among the extremist communist groups in Nepal from whom the Maoists emerged have been identified in the chart attached at the end as Annexure–I.

---

1   For Prachanda's early life and political career, see Pratik Pradhan and Ameet Dhakal, "Uncovering Prachanda...", *Kathmandu Post*, 8 April 2003.

The Maoists and other extremist Communist groups played an active role in the Peoples' Movement of 1989–90. They did not join the United Left Front, formed under the leadership of the mainstream Communist parties. Instead, they operated under their own umbrella organization called United National People's Movement (UNPM). It must be borne in mind that even during this movement, they were clearly and assertively demanding for the abolition of monarchy and the declaration of Nepal as a Republic. They were not happy with the compromise on a multi-party democratic system under Constitutional Monarchy that ended the Peoples' Movement against the partyless panchayat system in May 1990. They stood for a Constituent Assembly to draft a national democratic constitution. They were forced to accept the 1990 compromise as a 'first step' — 'the necessary capitalist revolution coming before the revolution and the final establishment of the true democracy in Nepal'.[2]

In pursuance of this demand, they were not initially inclined to participate in the general elections of May 1991 for a multi-party Parliament under the new Constitution of November 1990. However, they changed their position, perhaps with a view to changing the system by working from within. For this, they formed a two-tiered organization, of a revolutionary and a political front, known as Communist Party of Nepal–Unity Centre and the United

---

2 As told by Dr Baburam Bhattarai, to William Raeper and Martin Hoftun, *Spring Awakening: An Account of the 1990 Revolution in Nepal*, Viking, New Delhi, 1992, p. 34.

People's Front of Nepal (UPFN), respectively. An analyst summarising the tactical shift on elections made by the UPFN said that the Front was "willing to contest elections in order to gain a platform to 'expose' the inadequacy of the parliamentary system but rejects the goal of securing a parliamentary majority".[3] Realistically, it was not even possible for the Maoists to secure a majority and capture power through a democratic electoral process. The political front, i.e. the UPFN, participated in the elections of 1991. They put up 69 candidates and won nine seats, polling 4.83 per cent of the votes cast. Of these nine seats, they won four in the Western region (three in the two districts of Rolpa and Rukum), two in Kathmandu, two in the Terai and one in the Central region.[4] They emerged as the third largest group after the Nepali Congress and the Communist Party of Nepal (UML). The UPFN also performed impressively in the local bodies elections of 1992 by capturing a number of seats in various Village and District Development Committees.

However, the UPFN did not prove to be a cohesive front. After the 1992 local bodies elections and in the course of functioning within the Parliament, the egos and ideologies of the leaders clashed. There were attempts on the part of factions to dominate the organization, the Unity Centre

---

3 John Welpton, 'The General Elections of May 1991', in Michael Hutt (ed), *Nepal in the Nineties: Versions of the Past, Visions of the Future*, Oxford University Press, New Delhi, 1994, pp. 58–59.

4 Election Commission, *Pratinidhi Sabha Nirvachan, 2048*, (Election for the House of Representatives, 1991), Kathmandu, 1991.

disintegrated and the UPFN got split into two factions led by Nirmal Lama and Niranjan Govind Vaidya on the one hand and Dr Baburam Bhattarai and Pushpa Kamal Dahal-Prachanda on the other. It is the latter group that represents the Maoist insurgency in Nepal.[5]

The UPFN led by Lama and Vaidya succeeded in securing recognition of the election commission for the 1994 election and also participated in those elections, but the other group led by Baburam and Prachanda was not recognised as a separate party. Baburam took the case to the Supreme Court where the judgment took time until the completion of the mid-term poll. The Baburam group, being

---

5 The account of the early stages of the Maoists evolution is based on; R.S. Chauhan, *The Political Development in Nepal 1950–1970*, Associated Publishing House, New Delhi, 1971; R.S. Chauhan, *Society and State Building in Nepal*, Sterling Publishers, New Delhi, 1989; Bhim B. Rawal, *Nepal Ma Samyabadi Andolan: Uddhav Ra Bikas (Communist Movement in Nepal; Emergence and Development)*, Pairabi Prakashan, Kathmandu, 1991; Sridhar K. Khatri, et.al., *Political Parties and Parliamentary Process in Nepal: A Study of the Transitional Phase*, Political Science Association of Nepal, Kathmandu, 1992; Pancha N. Maharajan, "Role of the Extra-parliamentary Political Party in Multi-party Democracy: A case Study of the CPN–Unity Centre", *Contributions to Nepalese Studies*, Vol. 20, No. 2, Kathmandu, July 1993; Pancha N. Mahajan, "The Maoist Insurgency and the Crisis of Governability in Nepal" in Dhriba Kumar (Ed), *Domestic Conflict And Crisis of Governability In Nepal*, CNAS, Centre for Nepal and Asian Studies, Tribhuwan University, Kathmandu, 2000, pp. 163-187; Krishna P.Khanal et al., *Nepal: People, Polity and Governance: A Survey Analysis of People's Response to the Democratic Experiment (1991–95)*, Kathmandu, 1996; Krishna Hachhsthu, *Party Building in Nepal*, Mandala Book Point, Kathmandu, 2002.

not qualified to participate in the elections, boycotted them "as a face saving" response and also gave a call to all others to do so.[6] In 1995, this group called itself as Communist Party of Nepal (Maoist) and went underground. However, this Maoist group did not stop at boycotting the elections: in the areas of their influence and dominance, like Rolpa, Rukum, Jajarkot and Salyan, they started attacking landlords and government functionaries as also those voters and political activists who had taken part in the election process. The unleashing of violence by the Maoists was also a retaliation against the severe police action against their activities under a military operation code named 'Romeo' during 1994–95. On 13 February 1996, the Maoists declared their People's War (PW) in Nepal by attacking and looting a bank in Gorkha and three police posts in Rolpa and Rukum.[7]

This background to the rise of Maoists insurgency raises one question, i.e. was it possible to keep the Maoists functioning within the system as a mainstream political formation? There is no doubt that the Baburam and Prachanda group had committed itself to the extreme left ideological position including the "new democracy" of Maoist thought, but they could be pursuaded to carry on their ideological programme within the democratic and

---

6 Maharajan in Druba Kumar volume, op. cit. n. 3, p. 168.
7 Anand Swaroop Varma, *Rolpa se Dolpa Tak* (From Rolpa to Dolpa: Nepal's Maoist Movement), Contemporary Third World, NOIDA, India, February 2001.

peaceful framework. After all, they did participate in the 1991 elections and were inclined to do so in 1994 as well. Reiterating his faith in democratic ideals and peaceful methods, Baburam said:

> We want real new democracy which gives power to the oppressed, the peasantry and the poorest of the poor living in the villages. How, then, can people say that we are against democracy and that we are terrorists? Only if the government tries to resist democracy with arms we are duty-bound to do the same. We don't use arms on our own but we do retaliate. Terrorist are those who do not believe in the people's power.[8]

There surely is exaggeration and diversion in the claims made by the Maoist leader, but the fact remains that the other group of the UPFN, led by Lama and Vaidya, which got recognition in 1994 to participate in the elections, has continued to remain within the confines of the post-1990 Constitutional and political system. Unintentionally, perhaps the system created conditions for the marginalization of Baburam and Prachanda group and forced them to work from outside the system. Earlier in 1992, when they were a part of the larger UPFN and were represented in the parliament, they had submitted demands to the government

---

8   As quoted in Raeper and Hoftun, *Spring Awakening,* op.cit, p. 34.

and also carried out a Nepal bandh (country-wide strike) in April 1992. This strike precipitated a crisis for the government as a result of the killing of 16 people by the police while resisting the demonstrations. The resignations of Prime Minister Koirala and Home Minister Sher Bahadur Deuba were demanded during the strike. The government diffused the crisis by reaching a negotiated settlement with the CPN-UML, the main opposition party, but without any talks with the UPFN leaders. This kind of political marginalisation was not desirable in a multi-party democratic system. The Maoists also felt that the elected governments were using the state machinery, including the police force, to harass them and contain them politically, particularly between 1991–94. We have mentioned the "Operation Romeo" against the Maoists in 1994–95, which had the support of both mainstream parties, the Nepali Congress and the CPN-UML. An international report on Nepal underlining the harshness of the "Operation Romeo" says:

> ... efforts directed by the Congress Party leadership to suppress leftist political activity in the mountainous West, including through violent means such as the police-led Operation Romeo, only galvanized both the Maoists and a rising tide of localized resentment. An international official noted, "the police reverted to the way they had behaved during the *panchayat* era because they had no other framework of experience", and even a senior Nepalese government official agreed

that Operation Romeo was little more 'than the use of police for looting'. These heavy handed police operations are widely seen in retrospect as a disaster that provided vital fuel for the insurgency movement.[9]

---

9   *Nepal Backgrounder: Ceasefire — Soft Landing Or Strategic Pause?*, International Crisis Group (ICG), ICG Asia Report No. 50, Kathmandu/Brussels, 10 April 2003, p. 4.

II

Support Base and Political Goals

When we look at the support base of the Maoist Movement, the significance of the Western region is highlighted. Anti-feudal sentiment has been strongest in this region because of its political economy. This region is poorest and most underdeveloped, and is also inhabited by tribal and backward social groups who have felt exploited and discriminated against at the hands of the upper castes. Extremist Marxists like Mohan Bikram Singh and young rebels like Dr Baburam Bhattarai come from this region. Baburam's Ph.D. dissertation on 'Regional Development in Nepal' also made him conscious of the poor living conditions of this region. Kathmandu-based think-tanks have produced studies that show that the Western districts are "the worst in terms of child literacy, child labour, landless households and per capita food production".[10] A large section of these people also go as migratory labourers to India and the economy of the region is sustained by the remittances sent by them.

The Maoists' roots have been in the Western mid-hilly region but in the course of the past few years, these roots

---

10 Bertil Lintner, "Nepal struggles to cope with the diehard Maoist violence", *Jane's Defence Weekly*, June 1999, p. 43.

have expanded fairly, speedily to other areas in the central and eastern regions of Nepal, particularly in the mid-hills. At the time of their first attacks on the army in November 2001, it was estimated that the Maoists had strong support in about 44 of the 75 districts, particularly in the rural areas. Nearly 40 districts are shown as 'highly affected'. The districts where more than 50 deaths were recorded as a result of the Maoists' activities were Rolpa, Rukum, Jajarkot, Salyan and Kalikot, all in the Western mid-hills and Sindhuli and Kabre in the Eastern mid-hills. We have noted earlier that the eastern region witnessed the rise of Maoists violence, of the *Jhapali* group, during the early 1970s. The headquarters of the 'Maoist government', established in November 2001, is in Rolpa.

The social groups that constitute the bulk of the Maoists support are from the Magurali combination of indigenous people (*jan jatis*), i.e. Magars, Gurungs, Rais and Limbus. Besides them, the Kiratis, other Dalit groups and the Tharus of Terai have also joined the Maoists. Most of the tribals and Dalits are non-Hindus (Buddhists, atheists or animists), as well as non-Nepali speaking groups. They have their indigenous culture and want to preserve it rather than being dominated by the majority Hindu community. They approximately constitute 35 per cent of the kingdom's total population. Drawing attention to these people, the Maoist leader Baburam Bhatarai says:

The oppressed regions within the country are primarily the regions inhabited by the indigenous people since time immemorial. These indigenous people dominated regions that were independent tribal states prior to the formation of the centralized state in the later half of the eighteenth century, have been reduced to the present most backward and oppressed condition due to the internal feudal exploitation and the external semi-colonial oppression. They have been left behind by the historical development process.... Thus it is quite natural that the question of regional oppression of Mongol dominated eastern, central and western hilly regions or the Austro-Dravid dominated Inner Terai and Terai regions are manifested in the form of national oppression. There the regional and the national questions have intertwined with one another. Besides this, the problem of the Khas dominated far western Karnali region can occur as regional question, instead of a nationality question, and it will have to be tackled accordingly. Thus according to the concrete situation, it is necessary to solve the problem of oppressed regions and nationalities by granting regional and national autonomy.[11]

This is endorsed and reinforced by the top Maoist leader Prachanda who says:

Along with the developments of the people's war, a new consciousness fighting for their own rights and

---

11 Dr Baburam Bhattarai, *Politico-Economic Rationale of People's War in Nepal*, Monograph, 1998, www.icpnm.org. This monograph was also published in Kathmandu by Utprerak Publications Pvt. Ltd.

liberation is spreading amongst many oppressed nationalities of the country such as Magars, Gurungs, Tamangs, Newars, Tharus, Rais, Limbus and Madhesies. People's War has speeded up the formation of various national liberation fronts and expansion of nationality organizations. Similarly today, along with the development of People's War, a wave of organization and struggle has been created among Dalit castes at a great speed and a wider scale. Dalits are today rebelling against inhuman tyranny perpetrated upon them by the feudal state of high caste Hindus.[12]

While Prachanda's statement clearly underlines the organised support of tribal and Dalit groups, some observers contend that tribal and Dalit support to the Maoists is on voluntary and individual basis. The organizations officially representing the nationalities, and so recognised by the government of Nepal, have not publicly and politically identified themselves with the Maoist movement, particularly because its leadership is with the upper castes, as both Baburam and Prachanda are Brahmins. Underlining this aspect, Deepak Thapa contends:

… after initially flirting with the Maoists, the leadership of many ethnic groups has begun to argue that Nepali

12 As quoted in Krishna B. Bhattachan, "Possible Ethnic Revolution or Insurgency In A Predatory Unitary Hindu State, Nepal", in Dhruba Kumar volume, pp. 135–162. Also see "Great Leap Forward", *The Hindustan Times,* 21 April 2001.

Maoism may not be the answer to the challenge of communal discrimination, for the state power will likely remain with the upper castes, no matter how the contest ends. In this reading, the Magars of western hills who have died in disproportionate numbers in the People's War are no more than cannon fodder.[13]

There may be a point in the caste distinctions between the top Maoist leaders and other cadres. This has been highlighted recently in what appears to be officially sponsored mobilisation of indigenous communities and Dalits asking for redressal of their victimisation in Maoists' violence when the Maoists negotiating team had already arrived in Kathmandu in April 2003. But it should not be stretched too far because indigenous and backward people are also adequately represented, and are in the forefront of the movement at every level of the organization including the Central Committee and the Politburo. The Maoist leadership has consistently and quite forcefully emphasised the question of the rights of the indigenous people and the backward castes, and consciously mobilised them as the solid support base of their movement.[14] The nationalist

---

13 Deepak Thapa, "Day of the Maoist", in *Himal-South Asian,* Kathmandu, August 2000.
14 See, for instance, the documents of the National Convention of United Revolutionary People's Council (UPRC), held in September 2001 which underlines the representation of "oppressed nationalities, depressed regions, depressed castes and mass organizations" in the 37 member Executive Committee of the UPRC, *The Worker,* Organ of the CPN (Maoist), No.7, January 2002, p. 10.

organizations continue to make their demands and agitate against the government of the day. The post-4 October, 2002 government of the King, headed by Lokendra Bahadur Chand as Prime Minister, has claimed to have made attempts to woo some of the organizations representing backward castes and 'nationalities' in the hope of depriving the Maoists of their support.[15] This indirectly underlines the fact that nationality and backward groups are indeed, under the Maoist's influence. Without this support the Maoists could not expand so fast in the areas dominated by these social groups.

The professional groups that are the backbone of the Maoist Movement are teachers and students both in the rural as well as urban areas. They not only propagate the Maoists programme and agenda, but also actively participate in the strikes. The All Nepal National Independent Student's Union (Revolutionary), popularly known as ANNISU, which is supportive of the Maoists' claims a membership of 600,000 ranging from school children of age 9 and above.[16] Both the students and the teachers add an

---

15 Speaking at a programme of Tharu Students Society and the Tharu Kalyankarini Sabha, Prime Minister Chand said that the "development of all nationalities is the prime need of the day". In that meeting the Tharu leaders demanded the establishment of Indigenous Nationalities Academy and introduce Indigenous Decade (1994–2004), "in order to rehabilitate the freed Kamaiyas and stop the Tharus from falling prey to both the security forces and the Maoists". The Tharus have been the original inhabitatnts of 22 districts from the east to the west of the country. *The Rising Nepal*, 16 January 2003.

16 Paul Harris. "Riots, bombs and strikes hit Nepal as Maoists' step up People's War", *Jane's Intelligence Review*, February 2001, p. 45.

intellectual dimension to the movement and provide an effective network and communication link between the leadership and the masses. The women's cadres constitute another significant dimension of the support base of the Maoists. Women also occupy important places of leadership in the military wing of the movement and they have helped the movement gather strong support from women in general.[17]

In addition to those living in Nepal, the Maoists also look towards the persons of Nepali origin living in India as one of the most important source of support for them. Dr Baburam Bhattarai, during his education in India, had worked with Nepali students and Nepali expatriates in India and had helped organise them. The All India Nepalese Students Association (AINSA) is a very active organization working in India under the influence of the Maoists. In his report to the Second National Conference of the CPN (Maoist) in February 2001, the Secretary General of the Party Com. Prachanda said:

> The Party has assumed the expatriation of millions of Nepalese in search of jobs in India as a significant characteristic of Nepalese society. In fact, the success of Nepalese People's War and revolution cannot be imagined if Nepalese dwelling in India are separated from it.... Nepalese front located in India has been

---

17 Verma, *Rolpa se Dolpa Tak*, op.cit, n. 6, p. 31. Also Com. Parvati, "The Question of Women's Leadership in People's War in Nepal", *The Worker*, No. 8, January 2003.

playing a role of far reaching importance in the process
of historic initiative of People's War and afterwards
in its total development process.[18]

The Maoists have systematically structured, ideologically
cultivated and consistently mobilised this diversified social
support. While landless peasants, workers and poor farmers
have been the mainstay of the movement, the Maoists have
identified lower middle classes like school and college
teachers, doctors, engineers, white collar employees, small
traders and artisans also as their natural sympathisers and
supporters. Even rich peasants and the national bourgeoisie
have also been seen as potential, though undependable,
sources of support to the movement.[19]

The ideological programme of "new democracy"
adopted by the Maoists and the demands made by them to
the government reflect the concerns of their support base.
Initially the UPFN made an eight-point demand in February
1992, which was enlarged to 14 points within a month.
While formally launching the movement in February 1996,
the Maoists presented to the government a charter of 40
demands. This charter of demands cover three areas, i.e.
demands related to nationalism, welfare of the people and
the basic living conditions of the people. The demands
related to nationalism are mostly concerned with Nepal's
relations with India. The Maoists ask for abrogation of the

---

18 *The Worker,* (Organ of the CPN-Maoist), No.7, January 2002, pp. 60-61.
19 Documents adopted at the Third Plenum of the Central Committee
    of the CPN (Maoist) in March 1995, as quoted in Verma, ibid,
    pp. 44-45.

1950 Treaty and the Mahakali (1996) Treaty. They want Gurkha recruitment in foreign armies to stop. In the area of domestic governance closely related to the people's welfare, they ask for a Constituent Assembly to draft a new Constitution for removal of Monarchy and the special rights and privileges of the King and the royal family of the Royal Nepal Army to be placed under the people's control and for Nepal being declared a secular, not a Hindu, State. As a means of improving the lives of the ordinary people, the Maoists have demanded that the land should go to the cultivator, there should be right to work, minimum wages for the industrial, agricultural and service sector workers, free education, control of corruption and all other requirements of good governance. (For the full list of these forty demands, see Annexure II, Section 3).

Of these demands, the Maoists underlined two or three as critical ones, namely: making Nepal a republic, i.e. the abolition of the monarchy; establishment of an interim government to hold elections for a Constituent Assembly, in order to draft a new Constitution. They dropped the demand for abolition of the Monarchy in the course of three rounds of talks with the Deuba government in November 2001. But that was a tactical move to get the government to accept other demands of an interim government and an elected Constituent Assembly. They calculated that the objectives of abolition of the monarchy and Nepal being declared a republican and a secular state could be pursued through the Constituent Assembly. Though it has not been specifically stated, there are firm indications that the Maoists want to head the interim government themselves, and do not want to leave these vital questions to be decided in the king's or the political parties' discretion. They suggest that the interim government should be headed by the people's forces, as was done during the 1990 revolution. Since this time the Maoists are in the forefront of the people's forces, they should take control of the interim government. Whether such a government will have representatives of the political parties and monarchy is not made clear, but in their subsequent reformulation of demands, they have asked for a round table conference of the 'old' and the 'new' powers, i.e. the king and the political parties as 'old' powers and themselves as 'new' powers. This means that the representatives of political parties, or even of the king, may be accepted in the interim government by the Maoists, but they themselves will hold the dominant position.

It may be in order hereto outline the external influences in the making up of the Maoists' ideological position and evolution of their movement. As noted earlier, the Chinese cultural revolution of the mid-1960s and the consequent Naxalite movement in India during the late 1960s and the early 1970s provided strong initial stimulation in the evolution of Maoist movement in Nepal. Com. Prachanda and his associates also recall the 'positive' contribution made by Pushpa Lal and his faction of the Communist Party of Nepal in the growth of the movement. In the Party documents, the influence and continued relevance of the 'Great Proletarian Cultural Revolution' (GPCR), launched in China under the leadership of Mao is underlined with respect and admiration, but it is emphasised that the party was "moving further ahead from Maoism and the GPCR".[20]

The international contacts of the Nepali Maoists expanded during the 1980s when they became a founding member of the 'Revolutionary International Movement' (RIM), along with the comrades from the US, Latin America and other parts of the world. The RIM has been a competitor of the Comintern (Communist International). The evolution and naming of the Nepali version of Maoism as *Prachanda Path* (Prachanda's Way) may have been inspired by Peru's *Sendero Luminoso* (Shining Path). Experiences of other Communist movements in Asia have also enriched the Maoist's ideological formulations and approach. Explaining this Com. Prachanda says:

In this context, RIM committee kept on playing important role in synthesising experiences of the world .... Among all of them, those of People's War in Peru, initiated by Communist Party of Peru led by Com. Gonzalo had been the highest and most important. Also, the documents and articles written by the Revolutionary Communist Party, the USA and its Chairman Bob Avakin played an important role in lifting the debate to a new height. At the same time, positive and negative experiences of armed struggles in various countries including Turkey, India, the Philippines, Bangladesh, Iran had been the agenda for direct debates and interactions.[21]

---

20 Com. Prachanda's Report at the Second National Conference of the CPN-Maoist. *The Worker*, January 2002, op.cit, p. 52.
21 ibid, p. 44.

Among the Indian Communist groups, with whom the Nepali Maoists admit of having "direct and continuous debate", names of People's War Group (PWG) and the Maoist Communist Centre (MCC), are specifically mentioned.[22] The Maoists of South Asia have tried to institutionalise their contacts developed through RIM. In June 2001, 10 Maoist parties and organizations namely; Purba Bangla Sarbahara Party (CC), Purba Bangla Sarbahara Party (Maoist Punerghatan Kendra), Bangladesh Samyabadi Dal (ML), Communist Party of Ceylon (Maoist), Communist Party of India (M-L) (Naxalbari), Communist Party of India (M-L) (PW), Maoist Communist Center, Revolutionary Communist Center of India (MLM), Revolutionary Communist Center of India (Maoist) and Communist party of Nepal (Maoist), got together to form a Co-ordination Committee of Maoist Parties and Organizations of South Asia (CCOMPOSA). The stated objective of this organization is to "Unify and co-ordinate the activities of the Maoist parties and organizations in South Asia". This organization has hailed the People's War led by the CPN (Maoist), and attacked "US imperialism in Afghanistan", "Hindu fascist BJP in India", and "threats posed by Indian expansionists to Bhutan and Bangladesh".[23] The CCOMPOSA also aims

---

22 Deepak Thapa, on Maoists Indian connection, in *Nepal Times* (Weekly), Kathmandu, 14–20 December 2001. On the Maoists with the fraternal groups in India, in the provinces of Bihar, U.P., Jharkhand, Bengal and Sikkim, also see, Sanjay K. Jha, "The Maoist Maze", *South Asia Intelligence Review*, Vol. 1, No. 14, 21 October 2002, pp. 4–6. www.satp.org.

23 Deepak Thapa, *Nepal Times*, see also his, "Day of the Maoists" in *Himal-South Asia*, Kathmandu, August, 2000. and Sanjay Jha, 2002.

at establishing a 'Compact Revolutionary Zone' (CRZ) that will join Nepal with the parts of India in Bihar, Jharkhand and stretching up to Andhra Pradesh to link up the areas under the influence of the PWG. This zone, if established, can become the base for launching a people's war in the whole of India and even South Asia. This networking with other South Asian Maoist Parties, particularly those in India, have surely provided required support to the Nepal Maoists in their current People's War.

While it is necessary to identify and understand the external ideological and organizational links of the Nepalese Maoists, we must clearly keep in mind that the Nepalese uprising is largely and authentically nationalist and the Nepalese Maoists are the most motivated, organised and powerful among their fraternal groups in South Asia. For instance, a number of Maoist groups in India have been operating for more than two decades in various parts, but there is no indication of their emerging as a system-threatening force. There is no evidence available that shows that the Maoists have either been prompted, encouraged or funded by any outside forces. Their external links do not make them dependent in their activities in Nepal though they may use their fraternal links outside Nepal, in India and elsewhere, to seek shelter, medical help, supply of arms and ammunition, publicity and even financial support. Their funding has come mostly from exactions, looting of Nepalese banks and contributions from Nepalese diaspora in places like Hong Kong and the US. According to one estimate, there collections through these sources may add up to somewhere between $64 million to 128 million.[24] There are reports of the Maoists of Nepal procuring arms through some of the insurgents groups of India and South Asia like the PWG, MCC, ULFA, BODO, KLO (Kamtapur Liberation Organization) and LTTE, though hard evidence in such cases is difficult to come by. Most of the money and arms used by the Nepal Maoists so far seem to have come from the looting of Nepalese banks and police and army's stores. They have also collected money through extortions and other coercive methods within Nepal. Some reports emanating in the Indian media also link the ISI of Pakistan with the Maoists, but in that regard too, there is no dependable evidence. The ISI may as well try and exploit the Maoists' violence to their advantage as it hurts India, but the Maoists are aware that their association with the ISI can prove counter-productive and suicidal for them.

The political goal of the Maoists is therefore very clear, viz., to capture power in the name of establishing 'new democracy'. The parameters of "new democracy" have been explained in the ideological programme, emphasizing the justice and equality for the backward, indigenous and suffering people of Nepal. These parameters are constantly being refined and articulated as the movement evolves, but the bottom line is that the "new democracy" will not have any room for the dominance of feudal forces, and

---

24 Bertin Lintener, "Nepal's Maoists Prepare for Final Offensive", *Jane Intelligence Review,* October 2002. Also his, "Maoist Moneybags", *Far Eastern Economic Review,* 24 October 2002.

'capitalist' democratic parties.[25] The Maoists are conscious of the fact that it may not be possible for them to capture total power and establish 'new democracy' in one go, even through the people's war, launched by them since 1996. Tactically therefore, they are willing to move in stages and accept to work within the 'capitalist democratic' framework but not under the monarchy. As such they are willing to have a multiparty system. In one of his interviews to an Indian English daily, Com. Prachanda, the supremo of the Maoists said: "We are definitely against one-party dictatorship. There will be full freedom to all the anti-feudal and anti-imperialist political parties in New Democracy".[26] The people's war has been launched by the Maoists since February 1996 to capture power and create conditions for "new democracy".

---

25 An outline of the economic policy, programme and process of the "New Democratic Revolution" can be found in Dr Baburam Bhattarai's article on "Politico-Economic Rationale of People's War in Nepal", op.cit.

26 Interview to Aunohita Mazumdar. The *Sunday Times of India*, New Delhi, 2 December 2001, p. 13.

III

Seven Years of Insurgency

It is for the last seven years, that the Maoists are waging a violent struggle in the name of 'People's War' (PW) for advancing their political goals. Two critical aspects of the PW deserve careful understanding, viz., its 'military line' and its strategy of forging a 'united front'. On the military line, the PW is envisaged as a 'total war'. This 'total war' is defined by the Maoist leadership as:

Stress on rural works, but do not leave the urban ones, too; stress on the illegal works but don't give up legal possibilities, too; stress on certain strategic areas, but do not leave other areas, too; stress on the works of war, but don't leave the mass movements, too; stress on the underground works, but do not leave the over ground ones, too; stress on the rural class-struggle but don't leave the countrywide struggles, too; stress on the guerrilla warfare but do not leave the political propaganda and exposure, too; stress on the dissemination inside the country but don't leave the worldwide publicity, too; stress on the works of the formation of army, but don't leave the works of the formation of fronts organizations, too; stress on depending upon your organizations and forces, but don't give up actional (sick, operational/practical) unity and taking support, co-operation from international community, too.[27]

The Maoists are aware of the geographical limitation of no direct access to the sea or the possibility of a base in a neighbouring country for waging the armed struggle. However, the western and eastern hilly regions have been considered as providing ideal theatre. Accordingly, the PW and the regional military commands have been organized to be compatible with the east-west hilly region with their 'north-south flows'. The work on the strategy of waging war with the 'storm of the armed masses', and for this three-tiered military formations have been built up. They are: the militants or the main military force, which can be called the hardcore fighter force; the defence or the supporting and reserve force, and lastly; the volunteer groups, i.e. people's militia. There is a clear emphasis in raising a Peoples' Liberation Army (PLA), comprising of a permanent hardcore fighting force. Besides, there is also clear emphasis in building a 'base area', i.e. control of territory along with the guerrilla zone. The base area and the guerrilla zones have to be the 'areas of general action' and then the 'cities, including the capital, for propaganda zone'. The attempt of the leadership is to keep a harmony among these formations through the evolution of a synthesis

---

27 Prachanda's Report at the Second National Conference, February 2001, *The Worker,* January 2002. op.cit, p. 55.

between the controlled 'centralised planning and decentralized action' on the one hand and between political and military action on the other.[28]

It is difficult to make an approximate assessment of the armed strength of the Maoists. Speculative assessments range from 5000 to 8000 hardcore fighters, but they can even be more. After their latest effective operations in Jumla and Gorkha in the month of November 2002, Baburam Bhattarai answering a question on their army's strength and funding support , told *Washington Times* in an interview on 14 December 2002:

We have in recent months carried out highly successful military raids at district and zonal headquarters simultaneously in the Western and Eastern regions by brigade level formations of the People's Liberation Army. At the same time, we have conducted smaller raids, ambushes, sabotages, etc. in all the 75 districts of the country. We hope this will help you to make an intelligent guess about the strength and logistics of the PLA.

Since ours is a genuine People's War, the people themselves are the real source of our finances. We also collect taxes from businessmen and industrialists, and occasionally seize from banks. As regards the sources

---

28 These components of the Maoists military line have been developed through four extended meeting of the party where experiences gathered in the field have been integrated to develop new concepts and approaches. Ibid. pp. 54–56.

of weapons, it is an open secret that our enemy is the greatest source so far. As Mao said, even the foreign powers may supply us via our enemy.

The forging of 'united front' is the key to the Maoists' political strategy. Accordingly, they have kept their political moves flexible to isolate their worst adversary at a given point of time by joining hands with all possible other forces. Such alliances are changed when the main challenge to them shifts. Their flexibility is also reflected in their demands, such as the dropping of the demand for Republic, and also the occasional offer of cease-fire and negotiations. It must, however, be noticed that this flexibility is tactical to serve the interest of their basic goals. It helps them to regroup, project the image of being a reasonable and politically oriented organization and keep the initiative with them when conditions do not seem to be favourable.

Two instances may be recalled to illustrate the point. While launching the PW, the Maoists faced greatest challenge from the Nepalese governments headed by the mainstream political parties like the Nepalese Congress and the CPN-UML. Accordingly, during the period between February 1996 to June 2001, the main targets of the Maoists' violence were the NC and the UML cadres and political activists and supporters along with the key state functionaries. This was because the police operations against them were directed by the government headed by the political parties. During this period, they had a tactical understanding and tacit co-operation with King Birendra, who on his part, might not have been averse to let the

Bhattarai Maoists weaken and discredit the political parties. Baburam has admitted of having a "working unity" and under-standing on some principles with King Birendra.[29] An advantage of this working unity to the Maoists was that King Birendra dilly dallied the Koirala government's requests for the use of army against the Maoists, and also, the King did not approve, until 2001, the government's proposal for raising a new armed police force to fight the Maoists.

The Maoists have changed their tracks after the massacre of King Birendra and his family in June 2001, which led them to launch their first direct attacks on the Royal Nepalese army in November 2001. In the aftermath of the massacre of the Royal family, the Maoists described the new King as a 'murderer' and identified themselves openly with the slain King Birendra in order to harness popular support and sympathy. Particularly after King Gyanendra's take over on 4 October 2002, the Maoists have established contacts with the political parties and are now insisting on having a round table with the King, along with the political parties in pursuance of their objective of forming an interim government to hold elections for a Constituent Assembly.[30]

---

29 Prachanda's latest interview to *Janadharana Weekly*, (Nepalese), 19 December 2002.

30 Ibid., see also his article " Nepal: Triangular balance of Forces", in *Economic and Political Weekly*, (Bombay), 16 November 2002. His article *"Nepali janakranti ka kehi tatkalin prashna-haru* (Some Contemporary Questions of Nepalese People's Revolution", *Third World (Committed to the Oppressed Nations & People)*, Yr. 2, No. 2, May 30, 2002, pp. 5–8.

The Maoists are also in continuous touch with the various political parties to mobilize their support in driving hard bargain with the King.

The resilience in their approach is also evident with respect to the external dimension of their 'revolution'. For instance, two countries singled out for the strongest criticism in their debates and programme are the US and India. Soon after their attacks on the army pockets in November 2001, that escalated the civil war, the Maoist leadership has tried to reach the government of India to seek India's help, atleast by way of non-interference against their activities, in their struggle. They are conscious and politically sensitive to the fact that India is a critical factor not only in winning their struggle but also afterwards. Any substantial Indian intervention against their People's War (PW) can frustrate their goal of capturing power in Nepal and even after their capture of power, they may not be able to either stabilize themselves or carry out their political and economic programme without India's co-operation. For this tactical reason, the Maoists have also been sending messages to the US not to treat them as terrorists. They are also not averse to the possibility of external 'mediation or facilitation' by a 'truly independent and impartial force or organization', 'if necessary'.[31]

With the combination of their military line and political strategy, the Maoists have waged a ferocious war for the past seven years. Their violent campaign started

---

31 Dr Bhattarai's interview to *Janadharana* (Nepalese) Weekly, 19 December 2002.

systematically after the formal announcement of the People's War in 1996. Within two years, they established their military credibility, and their political influence and control grew in leaps and bounds. Even after absorbing a massive police onslaught through Operation 'Kilo-Sera-2', in 1998, they carried out successful raids in Dhanusha, Rolpa and Salyan districts. A major Maoist operation occurred in September 2000 in Dolpa district headquarters Dune Bazar which shook the confidence of the government forces. Until November 2001, all these operations were targeted against the armed police of Nepal. It is interesting to note that the Maoists did not attack the army, and moreover the RNA did not come to the rescue and protection of the police, like in Dune Bazar, it had been stationed at a distance that would barely take a 40 minutes'[32] drive. This was their gain resulting from their tacit understanding with the late King Birendra.

The first Maoist attack on the army came on 23 November 2001. Much had changed in Nepalese political situation since the Dolpa operations of the Maoists in September 2000. King Birendra and his family were assassinated in June 2001 in a ghastly incident in the Palace at the hands of Crown prince, who was himself killed by a bullet at the end of the drams. Gyanendra, King Birendra's brother became the new King. This was followed by the change: Deuba, leading a breakaway faction of the Nepali Congress displaced G.P. Koirala as Prime Minister. The Maoists termed the Royal Palace massacre as a conspiracy involving

---

32 Verma, *Rolpa se Dolpa Tak*, op.cit., pp. 22–33.

the new King, the US and India.[33] The new Deuba government initiated talks with the Maoists in August 2001, which had its third round in November. Soon after the third round, the Maoists walked out of the talks and launched widespread attacks on army and police posts in Dang, Pyuthan, Syangja and Surkhet districts causing extensive damage. They declared the setting up of a 37-member United Revolutionary Peoples' Council headed by Dr Bhattarai, with headquarters in Rolpa. These attacks also came after September 11, when almost the whole world had committed itself to fighting terrorism and the U.S. bombing of Afghanistan was still in progress.

The question that is generally asked is why the Maoists walked out of talks and escalated violence when international atmosphere was not favourable. One explanation offered in media circles widely in Nepal was that there were serious disagreements between the political and the military leadership of the rebels on the issue of talks with the government. Accordingly, the military wing, supposedly headed by Col. Ram Bahadur Thapa *a.k.a.* Com. Badal, launched the attacks on his own initiative to force the withdrawal of political leadership from talks.[34] The explanation sounds plausible, but one must keep in mind that Prachanda was the institutional head of both the political and military wings of the party. Further, even if there were differences, they did not affect the subsequent

---

33 Baburam Bhattarai's statement soon after the Palace events. Also see, ICG Asia Report No. 50, op.cit, p. 5.
34 See *Indian Express*, 2 December 2002.

military operations and the political line, because soon after these attacks, the political leaders issued several statements to justify their violation of ceasefire, withdrawal from talks and resort to military action. Their contention was that the government side was not willing, or even in a position to make a compromise for peaceful resolution of the problem. Instead, there were preparations by the army to launch their operations against the Maoists as there was no let-up in the government's harassment of the Maoists' cadres in villages and no releasing of those who were in prisons. According to Prachanda:

The Deuba government not only made nationwide preparations for military offensive but even banned the peaceful mass rallies. Even then we exercised maximum patience and proposed the convening of constituent assembly which was proclaimed even by King Tribhuwan after the Delhi Agreement of 1951, but never implemented.

The government not only rejected it but intensified the preparations of military offensive by procuring arms and ultra modern military helicopters from the US. In this situation of closing down of all political avenues, we had no alternative but to continue with the people's armed resistance.[35]

The Maoists therefore, took the advantage of a pre-emptive action and surprise. They were also feeling

---

35 Interview in The *Sunday Times of India*, 2 December 2002.

confident that they could now graduate from fighting the police to fighting the army after their battlefield experience of the past five years. There were reports of sophisticated automatic weapons being procured by the Maoists just a couple of weeks before the November 2001 attack took place.[36] Earlier, by February 2001, they had re-formulated and streamlined their military and political strategy to raise the PW to a higher level during the Party's second general conference.

Following the Dang attack, the Maoists inflicted another serious blow to the army in mid-February 2002 in Achem district. They suffered some set-backs in July, but then had again reinforced their prowess by the November 2002 operations in Jumla and Gorkha simultaneously. The early impressions and claims of the army that the Maoists will be soon subdued were subsequently being replaced by nervousness and a sense of despair. After the November operations, it became clear to everyone that the Maoists had an upper hand, militarily speaking. Politically also, they launched near-total strikes throughout the country and threatened to disrupt King Gyanendra's public reception in Biratnagar in January 2003. They did not actually carry out the threat, perhaps as a gesture to the government to lure them towards ceasefire and talks. This was a clear indication also of the fact that contacts had been established between the King's emissaries and those of the Maoists. The merciless killing of the Chief of the Armed Police Force,

---

36 Bertil Lintener, "Nepal Maoists Prepare For Final Offensive", *Janes Intelligence Review*, October 2002.

Krishna Mohan Shrestha and his wife days before the announcement of the ceasefire, perhaps was an indication that key personalities were now on their target besides the armed operations. As subsequent ceasefire announcement underlined, this killing could as well be aimed at hastening, rather than to stalling the beginning of ceasefire and talks.

In these seven-year long operations, the Maoists lost, until February 2001, some 1500 hardcore and other cadres. Included among them were the members of the Party's Politburo and Central Committee, high-ranking women cadres and even children.[37] After their first attack on the army in November 2001, Nepal has virtually been in a state of civil war. According to official estimates, in the last one year of this civil war, out of a total number of 4,366 persons killed, 4,050 have been Maoists. The Maoists assert that many of these people are civilians, killed indiscriminately by the army. There were reports that in some cases, the Maoists beheaded their slain leaders in the areas of operations to avoid their identification by the government forces. The killings were brutal and carried out without any consideration for human rights. The Party also faced considerable internal debate and bickering at various stages of military operations and on political issues, but the leadership claims that eventually these differences were resolved. In the course of the PW, women cadres have been repeatedly sexually exploited by their male

---

37 Com. Prachanda paid tributes to these martyrs in his report to the Second National Conference, *The Worker,* January 2002, op.cit, p. 26.

colleagues.[38] During the past one year of civil war, the Maoists have also attacked infrastructure like roads, bridges, power stations and even drinking water plants. In some cases, the Maoists have apologised for these attacks and promised not to target such facilities in future. They have also kidnapped school children, sometimes for forcible recruitment. Thus, the insurgency and the civil war have inflicted the worst kind of violence and disruption in Nepal, on a scale unprecedented in its history.

The Maoists have always been proposing talks and ceasefire as a part of their flexible strategy. The present round of ceasefire (2002–03) also serves their purpose as it will give them much needed time to regroup and recoup. This is necessitated by the fact that the RNA is not only being expanded but is also getting training and large arms supplies. The guns received from the US and in the pipeline from Belgium have been taken note of by the Maoists. Arms supplies have also gone from India in considerable quantities. As against this accretion of strength to the RNA, the Maoists have been facing problems in recruitment and ammunition supplies. There have also been signs of erosion in their support base due to continued and ruthless violence for more than two years. Commenting on the possible compulsions on the Maoists to ceasefire and start political negotiations, a former Maoist says:

---

38 This has been brought out in a recent study conducted by Nepal Women's Council on request from Maoist Women's group, *Kathmandu Post*, 7 February 2003.

The logistical challenge of managing its wildfire growth, supporting a brigade-strength fighting force on looted cash, the handicap of antiquated weaponry, the steady erosion of support from an intimidated countryside, and the possibility that the law of diminishing returns may have begun to set in with cadres getting restive over the failures in converting night-time strike missions into actual territorial gains — all these would have influenced the decision to engage in serious peace talks.[39]

The Maoists also perhaps have been approached by international agencies like the Red Cross, Amnesty and Norwegian and other western governments to stop violence. They even feel politically better placed to keep initiative with them with the differences between the king and the political parties sharpening since the king's 4 October 2002 take-over. And also at a time, when militarily they had an upper edge.

No less compulsions and need for ceasefire and talks have been that of the government of Nepal. Contrary to its tall claims that it will curb the insurgency in no time, the RNA has miserably failed to bring a semblance of order in the areas of its operations. The RNA has also failed in clearing areas of Maoist domination or snatch military

---

39   Pushkar Gautam, "The King's Ceasefire", *Himal* (Kathmandu), Vol. 16, No. 2, February 2003, p. 10. A detailed discussion of the Maoists' compulsions, for talks can also be found in, ICG Asia Report No. 50. op.cit, pp. 10–12.

initiative from them. In private conversations, it is admitted by the American officials and other independent observers that the RNA is ill-equipped to take on the Maoists effectively, and would take another year or so to reach that status of preparedness through the induction of new recruitments, more weapons and proper training.[40] The RNA is notorious for ruthless violation of human rights and indiscriminate killings and arrests. Politically, having taken over power himself, the King is under pressure to show results. The peace process can bring back the political initiative to him and help him rebuild his fractured legitimacy with the ordinary people who need peace and stability. Through peace process with the Maoists, the King can also keep the political parties at bay from seeking power again through the restoration of 1990 Constitution and of the dissolved Parliament, the latter demand being specifically made by the Nepali Congress. It is important to note in this respect that the government has yielded tactical ground to the Maoists in obtaining ceasefire by agreeing to withdraw the label of 'terrorists' from them, repeal the Act to combat and contain terrorism, cancel the red line notices for the arrests of Maoists leaders and cadres from the Interpol, to release some of their cadres, relax security checks and restrictions on their movements and withdraw the army and police force to their respective barracks.[41] There are indications that informally, the

---

40 Personal interviews.
41 See Baburam Bhattarai's article in *Nepal Samacharpatra*, 8 February
    2003.

government is inclined to have a round table discussion for the formation of an interim government as demanded by the Maoists though the government stoutly denies that they have agreed to any pre-conditions for ceasefire and talks with the Maoists.[42]

The only agreement between the two sides was on protection of 'sovereignty and nationalism' according to Col. Narayan Singh Pun, the Minister for Works and Physical Planning, who negotiated ceasefire with the Maoists.[43] On their part, the Maoists have agreed to call off their planned programmes of strikes and bandhs and stop attacking government installations. Whether Chief of Armed Police Force Krishna Mohan Shrestha's murder and attacks on customs department just before the announcement of ceasefire were planned as a signal to force the government in accepting the ceasefire were the results of differences within the Maoists on ceasefire, will remain a subject of debate and speculation. There could also be the possibility of a communication gap between the top leadership and local operatives in this regard because the leadership took time — about 10 days — to own IGP Shrestha's killing.[44]

---

42 Prime Minister Chand's assurances on this count to the CPN-UML leader Madhav Kumar Nepal. <nepalnews.com> 8 February 2003.
43 *Kathmandu Post*, 30 January 2003.
44 Baburam Bhattarai has owned it in his statement in *Nepal Samacharpatra*, on 8 February 2003.

IV

Response of the Nepal Government

The Nepal government's response to the Maoist challenge in general has been tardy, inconsistent and far from being effective. Under the system of constitutional monarchy adopted in 1990, the palace and the political parties are the two main political centres of decision-making. Both have adopted short-sighted approaches to serve their respective narrow political vested interests, thus creating conditions for Maoists to build themselves as a formidable political force. Looking at the monarchy's approach, the contrast is clearly evident in pre-July 2001 and post-July 2001 situations. King Birendra, as claimed by the Maoists had an under-standing with them and was instrumental in restraining the use of army against them. King Gyanendra unleashed the full force of the Nepalese state in suppressing the Maoist challenge, without desirable results. However, the possibility of the palace now trying to use (successfully or otherwise) the Maoists to discredit its political party detractors and also to retain as much power and influence as possible in any new political arrangement, cannot be ruled out. There are sharp differences within the King's cabinet on how to deal with the Maoists, but these are not very critical as the

King's direction will prevail. In a cabinet reshuffle on 11 April 2003, the King removed his Home Minister D.B. Thapa who was critical of ceasefire and talks with the Maoists. The sensitive portfolio of Home is now being handled by Prime Minister Chand himself, at least temporarily.[45] We shall come back to this issue in our concluding section.

The Nepalese governments led by the political parties over the past seven years have been equally erratic in dealing with the Maoists. The Nepali Congress has projected itself as a deeply divided organization where clash of personalities and conflict of sectional interests have defined policy approaches rather than the enlightened interests of either the organization, the democratic system, or the nation as a whole. The factions led by the veteran leaders G.P. Koirala and Krishna Prasad Bhattarai have torn apart internally the very organization that twice led struggle for democracy in Nepal and made innumerable sacrifices. G.P. Koirala when in power has preferred a law and order approach to counter the Maoists by force. And when he was doing so, his youger aspirant rival Sher Bahadur Deuba with the backing of Krishna Prasad Bhattarai had argued for a peaceful negotiated approach towards the Maoists. However, when in power, Deuba could not carry the process of negotiations to a logical conclusion and instead, called them 'terrorists' and vowed, "they need to be stamped out with all the might at our command. We will crush them,

---

45 *The Himalayan*, (Kathmandu), 12 April 2003; also *The Rising Nepal*, (Kathmandu), 12 April 2003.

whatever it takes; we will defeat them wherever they are".[46]
He was probably led by the post-September 11 anti-
terrorism context of international and regional situation.
He was also constrained by the role of the palace under the
new monarch, King Gyanendra, who, at least initially,
wanted to deal with the Maoists firmly. The other mainstream parties like the CPN-UML and the royalist Rastriya
Prajatantra Party (RPP) have also not been much different
from the Nepali Congress. Whenever in government, or
even in the Opposition, they have failed to project any
viable alternative approach for dealing with Nepal's most
serious security and political challenge during all these
years.

The broad thrust of the government's approach to the
Maoists was to treat them as a national security and a law
and order problem and deal with the use of force. We have
mentioned about the two major security operations of
'Romeo' and 'Kilo-Sierra-2' conducted by the police forces
in 1995 and 1998. They were very harsh and ruthless
operations with no respect for human rights. They managed
to physically eliminate a good number of Maoist cadres
but contributed to the strength and spread of the Maoist
movement. People in the areas of operation lost faith in the
government and developed sympathy for the Maoists who
were seen as victims of repression. In a very significant

---

46 *Indian Express*, 1 December 2001. On Koirala and Deuba approaches
to the Maoists, also see, Deepak Thapa, "Maoist Insurgency in Nepal",
Dialogue (A Journal of Astha Bharati), Vol. 4, No. 2, October–December
2002, pp. 89–100.

way, the Maoists' formal launching of the people's war was in retaliation to 'Operation Romeo'. These operations however, could not dent the rise of the Maoists as they were not adequate even in military terms, being launched by the police force. They led to a serious debate and tension within the government, between the elected government and the King in particular, on the use of army against the Maoists. We have mentioned earlier that the King did not favour the use of the armed forces as he thought that the army was not ready for it or that its long term consequences were not desirable for the country. The fact of King Birendra's tacit sympathies for the Maoists influencing his views in this regard cannot be ruled out. In a tension between the Prime Minister and the King on the question of using the Army, the decision-making structure also favoured the King. This decision could be taken only by the King on the recommendation of the National Security Council, which is constituted by the Prime Minister, Defence Minister and the Chief of the Army. Since G.P. Koirala was also his own Defence Minister, and the Chief of the Army Staff was directly loyal to the King, the National Security Council had a split vote and the King could have a decisive and final say in the matter. The King was forced to accept a parliamentary decision initiated by the Koirala government to raise additional armed police forces, but on the use of army he did not relent. The RNA did not enjoy a harmonious relationship with the police force and this continues to affect the overall efficiency of the Nepalese security forces in dealing with the Maoists.[47] This situation

---

47 ICG Asia Report No. 50, pp. 20–21, International Crisis Group.

changed only under the new monarch, King Gyanendra and that too because the Maoists had opened their operations against the army in November 2001.

In the post-November 2001 phase, the army initially claimed that it would blunt the Maoist challenge in a short time. It achieved some successes in Dolpa during April–July, but they were not lasting or adequate. The Maoists felt the pressure but they held on to their ground and soon took an edge over the army, as became clearly evident during the Jumla and Gorkha operations in mid-November 2002. The army ruthlessly violated human rights, raped women, carried out fake encounters, and killed the Maoist suspects held in captivity to show their success in operations so as to boost the morale of the forces, but the leadership knew that they were not getting anywhere.[48] The army claims to have recovered some of the money and property looted by the Maoists but this is in no way a dent in the Maoists operational capabilities. Accordingly, the army started blaming the political leadership, particularly the Opposition, for their own failures. They also put pressure on the government to postpone elections because they realized that almost 60–70 per cent of the rural areas were still under the control of the Maoists. The RNA has had some skirmishes and minor brush with insurgency and guerrilla operations during the 1960s, early 1970s and the late 1980s. But these were brief and sporadic encounters. They had no sustained experience of fighting either a regular

---

48 "Nepal: A Deepening Human Rights Crisis", London, December 2002, Amnesty International.

war or motivated and determined guerrilla operations. The army's strength was also not adequate with only 55,000 men and officers. The Maoists, mostly of the same ethnic composition as the lower rungs of the army, had spread widely in difficult terrain which army had never had a chance to map out earlier. They also did not have adequate and modern weapons or training to match the challenge.[49] The King's moves towards ceasefire and negotiations are a clear reflection of his government's realisation that the Maoists cannot be tamed militarily, certainly not yet.

The Maoists, as we noted earlier, have been consciously and consistently synchronising their military operations with political moves. No such organized thinking or planning is evident on the government side. There have been occasional references to the issues of economic under development and ethnic discrimination that lie at the root of the Maoist problem, but no concrete action has been taken on that count. In the past couple of months, the King's government has planned relief and rehabilitation prog- ramme at a cost of 500 million rupees in the Maoist-affected areas to erode the social base of the Maoists but this plan is still in the process of finalization. For funding this programme, the government has been appealing to its bilateral and multilateral donors for help.[50] Giving some

---

49 Deepak Thapa, "Erosion of the Nepali World", *Himal-South Asia*, April 2002. Some observations on Nepalese army can also be found in Gen. Ashok K. Mehta, "The Maoist Insurgency in Nepal", *Dialogue*, Vol. 4, No. 2, Oct–Dec, 2002. pp. 101–109.

50 *Kathmandu Post*, 12 November 2002.

details of this plan, Minister of Physical Planning and Works, Narayan Singh Pun said in January 2003:

> The government has finalized Disarm, Demobilize, Rehabilitate and Reintegrate (DDRR) programme and this will soon get Cabinet approval. The objective of the programme is to make the misguided Maoists realize that there is an alternative to war. Under this programme, to be supported by a number of donors, five camps — one each in five development regions — will be set up .... People who will give up insurgency will remain in the camps for six to eight months. They will receive training and other income generating skills so as to wipe out their war mindset, making them fit to return to their previous life.[51] The Asian Development Bank has now announced a concessional loan of $321 million over three years to support developmental projects in the conflict affected areas.[52]

The Chand government has also promised to make education free, in accordance with the Maoists' demand, but this has not invoked a positive response from the 'rebel students'.[53] In fact, the political record of the governments in Nepal, elected or otherwise, over the past four decades, has been so poor on governance and concern for the common man and the Maoist as well as royalists'

---

51 *Kathmandu Post,* 9 January 2003.
52 *Kathmandu Post,* 11 April 2003.
53 *Kathmandu Post,* 7 and 8 December 2002.

propaganda against the corruption, inefficiency and misgovernance of the political leaders has been so effective that the credibility of government to meet socio-economic needs of the Nepalese people is extremely shaky. The government has either not been able to start serious negotiations with the Maoists as in November 2000,[54] or it is just not in a position to show meaningful accommodation towards the political agenda of the Maoists, as during August–November 2001 parleys.

The government's, rather the King's most significant response to the Moaists has been the establishment of back channel contacts with the Maoists soon after the 4 October 2002, take over of power. These back channels in which King seems to have directly authorized one of the hand picked Ministers, Col. Narayan Singh Pun, without taking the Cabinet into full confidence, have yielded the ceasefire and promise of talks between the King and the Maoists of 29 January 2003. Since the declaration of ceasefire, two other related developments have taken place, namely, the 'Code of Conduct' (See Annexures), between the two sides to be implemented during the negotiations signed on 12 March 2003, and the first goodwill meeting between the two sides in Kathmandu on 13 April 2003. How these talks will proceed and what will they produce, remains to be seen.

---

54 Verma, op.cit, see "The Story of a Failed negotiation", pp. 51–55.

V

International Responses

The outside world did not really bother much about the Maoist insurgency in Nepal until November 2001 escalation of conflict. To a large extent, the attention of the US and other external forces to Nepal was the result of post-9/11 context in South and Central Asia. It is difficult to say if the international attention would have been drawn to Nepalese Maoists at all, even after the November 2001 if September 11 had not occurred.

In many significant ways, the Maoists are not terrorists to be covered under the 'war against global terrorism'. They have had no links with Osama bin Laden and the Taliban. They have a specific political agenda and the PW, under which the armed rebellion is being carried out, is a part of their ideological struggle. Such rebellions have existed both before and after 9/11. The Maoists can be seen as international rebels in their approach since they seek to co-ordinate their activities with like-minded ideological groups and they indeed claim to have a programme to liberate the poor and suppressed peoples all over the world. Their programme in South Asia, particularly involving Nepal, India, Bangladesh and Sri Lanka has been clearly defined as noted earlier. They also have international links in other countries including America and Europe. And yet, the post-9/11 framework of 'war against global terrorism' would not justifiably apply to them.

Soon after the November 2001 escalation of PW, support started pouring in to the government of Nepal in its fight against the Maoists from various countries. Looking at the regional and strategic context of Nepal, support from three sources, viz., China, the US, UK and their Western allies, and India, matter most. The Chinese government had, even before the present escalation, distanced itself from the Maoists saying that they were neither following Chairman Mao's ideology and philosophy nor the Beijing government have any sympathy for them. In view of the Chinese government, Mao's thought was China-specific and had no relevance to Nepal. The Chinese government expressed its concern at the sudden escalation of violence in the country and pledged all its support to the government of Nepal in dealing with the Maoists' activities.[55] China, however, did not label the Maoists as terrorists but called them 'revolutionaries' and has been periodically cautioning the Nepalese government not to seek external involvement in dealing with them. This caution is in reaction to the growing US presence in the Kingdom that the Chinese do not see as desirable either for Nepal or compatible with their interests in Nepal.

---

55 Statements of the Chinese Ambassador in Kathmandu, *The Rising Nepal*, 30 November and 20 December 2001; *Kathmandu Post*, 3 September 1999. Also <www.nepalnews.com> 29 November , 11 and 19 December 2001.

The most notable aspect of external support to the Nepalese government has come from the US, the UK and some of the European countries. The Swiss government was sponsoring a workshop on 'conflict management', which was expected to be attended by representatives of the Maoists, political parties and the King's government.[56] Among the international organizations, the UN, UNHCR and the ICRC (International Committee for Red Cross) have actively got involved in the peace related activities between the Maoists and the government. The ICRC wanted to have a dialogue with the two sides to improve living conditions of the ordinary people — "restore freedom of movement for people and goods and improving civilian security" — in the conflict zones.[57] The UNHCR intervened with the Government of India on the question of deportation of a Nepalese Maoist to the Nepalese government from India.[58] The UN, through its Resident Representative in Nepal, Dr Henning Karcher, directly and publicly offered to 'broker peace' between the government and the Maoists, as early as in October 2002. This was the first time an international organization had done so after the King's takeover of power.[59]

Though donors pleaded for peace, they also pledged support to the Nepalese government in fighting insurgency. All the donors of Nepal held a conference in London in

---

56 <http://www.nepalnews.com>, 10 February 2003.
57 <nepalnews.com>, 16 January 2003.
58 *Kathmandu Post,* 8 November and 8 December 2002. Also <nepalnews.com>., 11 November 2002.
59 <kantipuronline.com>, 23 October 2002.

2002, where it was decided to pool joint efforts to help Nepal get out of the current crisis. The US and the UK have been the driving force behind this conference. They have established at least three multilateral committees of defence and security, political issues, and economic and developmental issues to fund and monitor these areas. It may, however, be noted here that the European donors always emphasized the peace and humanitarian aspects. Norway also expressed strong concern on the destruction of infrastructure and even threatened to discontinue assistance if violation of human rights was not stopped and the democratic process was not resumed.[60]

The US and UK were comparatively more emphatic on combating insurgency, and they seem to be working in tandem. Senior foreign Ministry officials have visited Nepal to take cognizance of the situation directly. This included the US Secretary of States Gen. Colin Powell (February 2002) and the British Under Secretary of State in the Foreign and Commonwealth Office Michael Jay (December 2002). These visits were the first visits in many decades at such high levels. Both Powell and Jay pledged strong military and economic support of their governments to Nepal in fighting the Maoists. The UK, due to its sizeable influence in the Nepalese army and the retired British Gurkha troops, has also been believed to be behind the peace moves in Nepal. The government of the United Kingdom also appointed a special representative, Sir Jeffrey James, to facilitate the

---

60 *Kathmandu Post*, 6 December 2002; also 28 January 2003.

proposed peace talks between the Maoists and the government. This was done, according to British diplomats in Kathmandu, at the initiative of Prime Minister Tony Blair and not on the request of the Nepalese government.[61] It may be of interest to keep in mind here that while the Maoists wanted a third party involvement in the peace process, may be to secure international legitimacy for themselves, the King was averse to this idea.

The US involvement in Nepal has been more active, visible and unprecedented. The Assistant Secretary of State Miss Christina Rocca has visited Nepal thrice in 2002, and has been in direct contact with the King and the armed forces. In her last visit, she reiterated the US government's resolve; "We are committed to help Nepal combat the insurgency by providing security assistance to the Nepalese government. Assistance will be provided in the form of a package including equipment, supplies and training for the Nepalese security forces".[62] It may useful to keep in mind that this visit took place after the Maoists had killed two of the Nepalese security guards of American Embassy alleging them of indulging in espionage and they had also threatened attacks on the Embassy. Reacting strongly to such threats, the US issued a travel advisory for the Americans against visiting to or moving freely in Nepal. The US has, however, not yet formally designated the Maoists as terrorists. Answering a question on this issue, Ms Rocca said: "... this

61 *Kathmandu Post*, 1 March 2003.
62 For reports of her last visit in December 2002, see, *Kathmandu Post*, 14 and 15 December 2002.
63 Ibid.

step may be taken in consideration if their violence continues unabated".[63] This also indicates that the US, while helping the King's regime militarily, was also trying to explore the possibility of opening negotiations with the Maoists. A junior State Department official, Donald Camp, claimed that ceasefire and proposed talks between the King and the Maoists announced in January 2003, were "a success of the US policy" and that the US will not allow the Maoists to prevail".[64] This US position has again been reiterated by Camp's boss Ms Rocca again recently when in a statement before the US Senate Committee on Foreign Relations in Washington, she said:

> We believe the parties have come this far only because the RNA was able to make an effective stand — a goal which U.S. security assistance aims to bolster .... In co-ordination with Great Britain, India and other partners, our security assistance will provide directly needed arms, equipments and training to enable the Royal Nepal Army (RNA) to counter the Maoist military threat.... (the US) also support efforts to bolster government control in areas vulnerable to Maoist influence by funding high-impact rural infrastructure and employment projects.[65]

---

64 For Deputy Assistant Secretary Scott Camp's statement at Heritage Foundation, see <nepalnews.com> , 4 March 2003. Also see the report on this subject in *Nepali Times*, No. 135, 7–13 March 2003.
65 *Kathmandu Post*, 28 March 2003.

The notable aspect of the US position on the Maoists question is that there is a great deal of backing provided to the RNA and the King's post-4 October 2002, notwithstanding occasional reference to democracy. The US neither disapproved of the King's take-over of direct power in violation of the 1990 Constitution, nor has the US asked the King to carry Nepalese political parties with him so as to effectively and politically deal with the Maoists.

It may be of interest to note here that after the early 1960s, direct military assistance by the US to Nepal has transpired for the first time. The arms supplied by the US include MI-16 AZ rifles, helicopters, twin engine STOL aircraft, ammunition and other non-lethal weapons. The quantum of military assistance actually received was reduced from $20 million initially promised during the then Prime Minister Deuba's visit to the US in May 2002, to $12 million. This has naturally disappointed the Nepalese security forces. The reasons advanced for this reduction are "budget stringencies and shifting priorities in the war on terrorism".[66] Perhaps the indications of the coming ceasefire and caution sounded by other donors, as well as India, regarding not strengthening Royal Nepal Army, and hence monarchy, against other democratic forces might also have weighed on the US administration.

The possibility of the US having long-term interests of a strategic nature in Nepal cannot be ruled out. There were reports of the seeking Nepal's co-operation in setting up a military observation post in northern areas, possibly in the

---

66 *Kathmandu Post*, 2 January 2003.

Mustang region bordering Tibet, where the US intelligence agencies had trained and used Khampa tribals for organising raids in Tibet between 1960–1974. Speculation in this respect was raised during Deuba's visit to the US, but the reports were strongly denied by the US Ambassador in Kathmandu Michael Malinowski, saying that such reports were "erroneous, uninformed and foolish".[67] The Defence Ministry, however, separately disclosed that an American military assessment mission was invited to Nepal to assess military requirements in the context of Maoists' threat.[68] This team of about a dozen experts and officers came in April 2002, and visited the areas affected by the Maoists insurgency, including the parts of northern region. It is believed in Kathmandu's media circles that Nepal has developed cold feet on this proposal of setting up a military post, under the Chinese pressure. There may also be strong reservations on any such proposals. The Maoist leader Baburam Bhattarai comments that the growing US military presence in Nepal is in the long-term interest aimed at encircling China and containing India is significant.[69] Some corroboration of speculation in this respect was evident in Nepal government's recent decision to establish a seismic centre to monitor possible nuclear explosions in the region under Comprehensive Test Ban Treaty (CTBT) regime.[70] Nepal is not even a member of the International Atomic

---

67   <nepalnews.com br> 4 May 2002; *The Hindustan Times*, 5 May 2002.
68   <nepalnews.com br> 4 May 2002.
69   See Dr Bhattarai's article, "Some Current Issues of Nepali People's Revolution", in *Third World*, Yr. 2, No. 2, 30 May 2002.

Energy Agency as yet and its limited capabilities in respect of monitoring nuclear tests will allow this centre to be manned and managed by foreigners. The countries that this centre will keep an eye on are naturally China, India and Pakistan.

Besides supply of arms, the US has also started training Nepalese forces. The US military team visiting Nepal had suggested augmentation and upgrading of the Royal Nepal Army.[71] Along the US lines, the RNA has raised a "Rangers Battalian" of up to 1000 soldiers for commando type operation.[72] An estimated 40-member US training team from the Pacific Command has had a joint military exercise with the RNA. The stated purpose of this exercise was to "enhance operational capability, inter-operability with other forces and tactical efficiency of the host nation". But these US soldiers were working with the RNA in the Maoist affected areas.[73] The US has also extended a grant of Nepali Rs 390 million to strengthen human rights cell in the army, as increasing international concerns have been raised regarding human rights violations of RNA.[74]

70 Suvecha Pant, "Seismic Station to be setup", *Kathmandu Post,* 4 March 2003.
71 General Ashok Mehta, in *Dialogue,* October–December 2002, op.cit. p. 104.
72 *Kathmandu Post,* 12 February 2003.
73 *Kathmandu Post,* 14 January 2003.
74 <nepalnews.com>, 7 January 2003.

VI

India and the Maoist Challenge

Like most of the other countries, India also woke up to the Maoists' challenge in Nepal after the escalation of violence in November 2001. Until then, for nearly six years since the February 1996 declaration of the PW by the Maoists, the Government of India's approach to the possible threat arising from this insurgency was casual. Law and order being treated as a state subject, the Central government in India absolved itself of any responsibility in restraining and containing the activities of the Maoists along the Indo-Nepal border. Even the June 2001 establishment of a co-ordination committee of the South Asian Maoists was just taken routine note of by the Indian intelligence agencies without any policy decision at the political level.

In response to the November escalation, India even before the Nepalese government did, declared the Maoists as terrorists and promised all possible support to the government in Kathmandu. However, the actual delivery of the military assistance was allowed to be processed leisurely under the consideration that military support was likely to strengthen the RNA and hence, indirectly the monarchy at the cost of democratic institutions. Not much effective steps were also taken to restrict the free movement of the Maoists across the Indo-Nepal border. Nepalese and

Indian army chiefs and officers exchanged visits and assurances of support, but military hardware moved slowly. All this changed only when pressure started building from the Nepalese side through allegations that India was indirectly supportive of the Maoists, by letting them use Indian territory for shelter, sanctuaries and logistic help. King Gyanendra's visit to India in July 2002 was significant in this respect. By then, India was also getting concerned about the steady rise in the US and British military presence in Nepal. India had a written understanding with Nepal concluded in 1965, that Nepal could procure arms from third countries such as the Unites States and the United Kingdom, if India could not supply its requirements.

Slowly, it started dawning on Indian policy makers that the gradual spread and consolidation of the American and British military and political presence in Nepal was not a very desirable development in India's own long-term interests. India's Foreign Secretary Kanwal Sibal in his speech at the French Institute of International Relations in Paris on 17 December 2002, hinting at this concern said with regard to Nepal that: "Western countries should also be careful about extending excessive military assistance to Nepal in order to avoid increase in the lethality of internal conflict and leakage of arms to the Maoists."[75] India's reservations on the western donors' approach to the question of insurgency in Nepal became evident when it refused to join multilateral committees to monitor

---

75 *The Indian Express*, (New Delhi), 3 January 2003.

developmental, political and security issues in Nepal. India also showed its displeasure with the flow of third country arms into Nepal by delaying the over-flight permission to the American and Belgian guns. India also inspected these arms cargos to make sure that they did not pose any long-term threat to India's internal stability and security by these arms falling eventually into wrong hands.

Indian policy received a further set-back when a whispering campaign was let loose in Nepal blaming India of sheltering the Maoists, contrary to all that it was doing, including providing military assistance to Nepal govern-ment. Then came on 4 October 2002, the dismissal of the Deuba government and the takeover of direct power by the King. The puppet government installed by the King was seen as a breach of the principles of Constitutional Monarchy and the multi-party democracy, the two pillars of India's basic approach in Nepal. Subsequently, India also felt left out when suddenly on 29 January 2003, the King's government and the Maoists announced ceasefire and agreed to hold talks to resolve the problem of insurgency. Expressing resentment at this marginalisation of India, Foreign Secretary Kanwal Sibal said at a Track-II meeting of Indian and Nepalese participants where Nepal's Ambassador in India Dr B.B. Thapa was also present, that India was not taken into confidence and that there was no consultation from the Nepalese side on vital issues affecting bilateral relations between the two countries. He asked as to what was India expected to do in relation to the Nepalese Maoists: stop monitoring their movements across the borders and stop giving military support to the Nepalese government since ceasefire and talks have been announced?[76]

India cannot be absolved from its own responsibility in bringing itself to this state of marginalisation with regard to its concerns in Nepal. There are two serious problems with India's Nepal policy. One is that it does not recognise the fallacy of its two-pillar approach. There is a serious inherent conflict between the interests of multi-party democracy based on the concept of popular sovereignty and the King's political aspirations and self-perceived divine role to rule. Even in 1990, the co-existence between the King and the political parties was neither natural, nor sincere nor honest. A former Chief Justice of Nepal's Supreme Court and a member of the Constitution drafting Committee in 1990, Mr Vishwambhar Nath Upadhyaya opined that from the first day, the palace had not co-operated in proper execution of the 1990 Constitution. The two pillars of India's Nepal policy, the King and the political parties, have on various occasions found it difficult to work in harmony with each other, more so since Gyanendra's coming to power and particularly after the King's take over of October 2002.

It is unrealistic on India's part to continue to harp on the two pillar policy under these circumstances. It may also be not out of place to mention here that political parties are fraught with internal conflicts, lack of credible leadership, failure on account of governance and erosion of

---

76 For his statement see *The Hindu*, 17 February 2003.

ideological and political integrity to lead Nepal out of the present crisis. The monarchy on its part, since the first political coup by King Mahendra against the representative government in December 1960, built its political base by pursuing policies that have been incompatible with India's legitimate and enlightened interests in Nepal. The contribution of monarchy in shaping Nepalese nationalism along anti-Indian lines has been the single largest. This basic incompatibility of interests between India and the Nepalese monarchy had brought them into direct clashes not only during the periods of Nehru and Indira Gandhi's rule but also during Rajiv Gandhi's period, during 1988–89, which in a significant way, contributed towards the success of the people's revolution and anti-Panchayat movement of 1989–90.[77] There are, no doubt, socio-cultural and emotional constituencies in India that hold the Hindu monarch of Nepal in high esteem and there is also an intricate web of family ties at the elite level in India that the King nurses to ensure support for him. However, the monarchy as an institution has done precious little in accommodating India's legitimate security and economic concerns and interests in Nepal. Under the circumstances, it cannot be rationally explained as to why should India bank so much on Nepalese monarchy, even within the Constitutional framework and as a symbol of stability.

The other problem of India's Nepal policy in the present context is that it has failed to make a balanced and

---

77 For further details of these events see S.D. Muni, *India and Nepal: A Changing Relationship*, Konark Publishers, New Delhi, 1993.

dispassionate assessment of the Maoists. The Maoists have been seen by the Government of India as a serious security challenge to India's interests in more than one ways, viz.,:

- Generating instability in Nepal and creating conditions for intervention from outside powers.
- Networking with other insurgent groups in India and South Asia to create instability in the region. The establishment of a Coordinating Committee of Maoists Groups in South Asia in June 2001 provides an institutional structure for this purpose.
- Demanding a restructuring of India–Nepal relations, through revision or abrogation of some of the important bilateral treaties like the Treaty of Peace and Friendship of 1950, and the Mahakali treaty of 1996, and projecting India as an exploitative and hegemonic power in the region.
- Possible and potential links of Maoists with ISI, North-east insurgent groups, the LTTE, etc.
- The Maoists' use of violent and terrorist methods to capture power at the cost of democratic institutions and governance.[78]

---

78 See for instance, two USI Journal articles, Shri Nishchal Nath Pandey, "Nepal's Maoist Movement and Implications for India", and Major General Ashok K. Mehta, AVSM (Retd), "The Maoist Insurgency In Nepal: Implications for India", *Journal of the United Service Institution of India,* Vol. CXXXII, No. 550, October–December 2002, New Delhi, pp. 558–579. Also see, Puskar Gautam, "The King's Ceasefire", *Himal,* Vol. 16, No. 2, February 2003, Kathmandu, pp. 9–13.

All these concerns may seem valid on the face, but at least some of them need careful scrutiny. To begin with, there is no hard evidence to suggest that the Maoists are either inspired, funded or influenced by any of the foreign interests. The Maoists' violence has certainly facilitated the US and the UK to expand their respective strategic interests and presence in Nepal, but that could have happened even otherwise in the aftermath of 9/11 events under the impact of which strategic interests of the Western powers in Asia have been redefined, reinforced and vigorously pursued. Further, the credit for the consolidation of the Western presence should go to the King and the governments in Nepal, who have always looked with favour at any opportunity to encourage outside powers in Nepal to counteract India's stakes and presence.

The Maoists' opposition to the existing pattern of relations with India is clearly articulated and they also ask for the abrogation of the Treaties of 1950 and Mahakali, and other, if any, unequal Treaties. But then, Maoists are not the only or even the first to raise these issues in India–Nepal relations. Almost every political party in Nepal as also the King have done so on may occasions and at times, consistently in the post-Rana Nepal. The review and revision of the 1950 Treaty is almost a national demand of Nepal. It is unfair to credit or blame only the Maoists for this demand. The other insurgent groups in India and South Asia, particularly the PWG, the MCC and some of the North-east tribal and ethnic insurgents, have been operating much earlier than the Maoists came on the scene. Somehow the Government of India has evolved a pattern of its own to deal with these internal insurgencies and the Maoists can hardly make any significant difference to their activities. The possibility of the Maoists using these groups for procuring arms and other logistic support in their activities exists and has certainly been harnessed, and this is a cause of security concern for India as the arms may flow to Indian groups through these channels as well. However, the extent of security threat posed by this to India should not be unduly exaggerated to rationalise India's hostility to the Maoists. If this threat was so serious, why India took the emergence of the Maoists casually between February 1996 and November 2001. It also needs to be stated here that the spread and success of the Maoists in Nepal should be seen as a reflection of the political and socio-economic context there. The Naxalites, the MCC and the People's War Group can never attain comparable success in a democratically resilient and developmentally dynamic India that can keep ideologically inspired insurgencies contained.

Last but not the least, the Maoists, as any other political force in Nepal, realise that India is crucial for their struggle, victory or survival in power, if ever they were to come to power. Their anti-India rhetoric notwithstanding, they have tried to establish contacts and understanding with India, but without any response. There were also indications that the Maoists moderated and diluted their anti-India rhetoric between November 2001 and January 2003. India has refused to touch them with a barge of pole, ignoring the fact they have emerged as a powerful player in the Nepalese political context and represent support of a large section of its poor and oppressed masses in the mid-hill regions. After all, even the King whose abolition is the principal goal of the Maoists has agreed to deal with them, and the Maoists on their part, have shown a remarkable flexibility and pragmatism in their approach to monarchy. This possibility existed, and does exist even now, between India and Maoists as well, if the former sees this as worth exploring, in its own policy calculations. In fact, a practical engagement with the Maoists in Nepal cannot be avoided if India wants to see Nepal stabilized, its monarchy democratized and its internal autonomy preserved from the growing Western and other undesirable influences. There is a pressing need for Indian policy makers to re-assess the Maoists and recast their whole approach to the emerging situation in Nepal. There are too many cooks and diverse social and political interests in India's Nepal policy making process to let a sincere and dispassionate re-assessment take place, though the need for such a re-assessment is deeply felt in some foreign policy establishments.

A more realistic alternative for the Indian policy in Nepal is to alter its two-pillar policy of supporting the King and the democratic parties. Nepal stands at a junction where it could launch itself on the way to the evolution of a true democracy. India needs to get engaged with the ongoing peace process and help Nepal take a direction towards reinforcing democratic forces and institutions reflecting aspirations of the ordinary Nepalese. India cannot meaningfully get engaged with the peace process unless it gets constructively engaged with the Maoists. India's image in Nepal today is that it is an ally and supporter of monarchy. India needs to bring the Maoists and the political parties together which, in the process will also moderate the Maoists' extremist stance and use of violent methods. It is this combination of the mainstream political parties and the Maoists which can contain monarchy's powers, help India emerge as a people-friendly neighbour and reduce the excessive influence and strategic presence of the Western powers. This will also help India assume greater political initiative in Nepal during this sensitive and delicate peace process. An improvement in the rapport between India and the Maoists may also be helpful in moderating the activities of the left extremist forces within India.

VII

Prospects

The compulsions that drove the King and the Maoists to ceasefire and negotiations have been identified earlier. The indications are that the process of negotiations will move rather slowly, with tough bargaining inevitable at almost every stage. This is evident in the fact that within days of the signing of the mutually agreed 'Code of Conduct', each side is accusing the other of violating this code. Members of the Maoist negotiating team in the course of their public meetings allover the kingdom have repeatedly blamed the King for not adhering to the 'Code of Conduct' regarding releasing the central level Maoist leaders, and Minister Pun has accused the Maoists of 'increasing their demands' adding that the government is not bound to agree to all their demands'.[79] Chief of the Maoist negotiating team Dr Bhattarai has directly blamed the King for blocking the peace process. While the Maoist negotiating team was announced in the very first statement of the Maoists leader Prachanda on the ceasefire, the official negotiating team from the King's side was announced only on 16 April 2003, after considerable delay and speculation. As noted

---

79 Ghanshyam Ojha, "Seeds of doubt begin to sprout about peace process", *Kathmandu Post*, 8 April 2003.

earlier, the first contacts, for the 'good-will' talks, between the Maoist negotiators led by Baburam, and the King's side, represented by Minister Pun, took place on 13 April 2003. The government negotiating team is headed by the Deputy Prime Minister Badri Prasad Mandal. This team includes Col. Pun and four other ministers, including a woman minister Ms Anuradha Koirala. This indicates the direct involvement of the Cabinet in the peace process, that had not been the case thus far. This is not yet clear as to what brief, if any, the King has given to this team but Col. Pun's presence on the government side underlines that these talks will have some sort of continuity with the earlier contacts and the King will keep in touch with the pace and content of negotiations. The first contacts could be established only after the King's side had partially accommodated the Maoists' pre-condition of the release of five Maoists leaders, including the party's Central Committee members.

The peace process in Nepal is a delicate and complex one, but everyone seems to be having stakes in sustaining it, at least for the present. There are three possible directions that this peace process may take place. One is based on what has been termed as a 'strategic pause'.[80] Accordingly, either side will sustain the talks and the ceasefire as long as its strategic needs so demand. Here, the strategic needs would depend upon completing arms acquisition and training programmes, and making adequate recruitments by the RNA and the Maoists. Both the combatants would

---

80 The ICG Asia Report No. 50 of 10 April 2003, (op.cit.) on Nepal describes it as such.

also like to reinforce and expand their political constituencies and ensure continued help and co-operation from the international community for their respective positions. The extensive tours and public meetings addressed both by the King as well as the Maoist negotiating team during March and April 2003, may be taken note of in this respect. It is interesting that the King in his addresses to the people of the western region, the stronghold of the Maoists, emphasised the centrality of monarchy in Nepal's history and the bond of affection existing between the King and the people. He said in Dhangarhi on 3 April 2003:

> The quintessence of our Nepal identity is the strong bond between the institution of monarchy and the people nurtured by mutual affection and confidence. Nepal has been able to maintain her independent identity and self-respect throughout her history only because of the peoples' unwavering trust in the institution of monarchy and the monarchy's unqualified dedication towards the people...
>
> It is but natural to have differences of opinion and competition in a multi-party democracy. However, the converging point of all these different opinions must be patriotism. A monarchy ever devoted towards the country and the people and a people with an innate love for their land is the glorious past of Nepal history, its present and also its future.[81]

---

81 www.kantipuronline.org

If the purpose of ceasefire and talks on both sides is to use it as a 'strategic pause', then no substantive issues are expected to be brought on the table and no compromises and mutual accommodations are to be sought or extended. Talks will continue to take place slowly, in one form or the other, as long as either or both the parties are not prepared to get back to the conflict with greater confidence. The King seems to be assured by the US that he will be backed up to the hilt and the RNA's preparations and training programmes have only been stepped up.

The second possibility is that the 'strategic pause' is used by either side to out-manoeuvre the other politically. The King's side may over-stretch the negotiations without conceding anything substantially to the Maoists to encourage cleavages and divisions among the Maoists leaders as also between the leadership and the cadres. It may also try and lure the sections of the more pliable leadership through offers of money, office and other material or political advantages to break the leadership and disintegrate the movement. If that becomes possible, the RNA would find it easy to deal militarily with the sections isolated through this selective process of co-option. Perhaps, such fears have prompted the Maoists for postponing the talks indefinitely on 19 April 2003. To them, the delayed constitution and the composition of the King's official negotiating team shows the lack of seriousness on the part of the King. According to one assessment, the RNA is hopeful that once it has acquired sufficient quantities of modern weapons and reached a force strength of 70,000 men, it would be able to defeat the Maoists militarily.[82] Others speculate that the RNA will have to raise its manpower threefold, atleast 150,000, before it can be confident of taking on the Maoists.[83] It is believed that the King was briefing his Indian interlocutors along the lines that nothing much may come out of the talks and that the Maoists may not be able to sustain the process of negotiations, during his recent visit to India in March 2003. Sections of Kathmandu elites also suspect this to be the King's game plan. They seem to be in sympathy with the mainstream political parties' allegations that the King has been instigating splits and divisions in their ranks and files in order to weaken them and co-opt the pliable sections.[84] The only flaw in the King's strategy in this respect appears to be that he is not cultivating the mainstream political parties which is a necessary condition for isolating the Maoists in a triangular balance of power.

The Maoists on their part are mobilising support from the mainstream political parties and are also trying to establish their credentials with international community to isolate the King. The Maoist negotiating team has had talks with the leaders of all the mainstream political parties and

---

82 Ibid, p. 20.

83 Major General Ashok K. Mehta in *USI Journal*, October–December 2002, op.cit.

84 The latest of such allegations has been made by the UML leader Madhav Kumar Nepal saying that the King is trying to instigate splits within the parties because they have decided to launch a decisive movement against him for democracy. <nepalnews.com> am 19 April 2003.

sought meetings with the representatives of the EU, the US, the UK, China and India to explain their point of view. If the Maoists and the mainstream political parties decide to build a peoples' movement on the lines of 1990, the King can surely be outmanoeuvred. There are indications that both the Nepali Congress and the UML are getting round to this point of view, but reservations and opposition from within the ranks in each of the parties exist. They are preparing to launch a movement on these lines as they continue to be neglected by the King. The core of the mainstream political parties' approach may be to use the Maoists' pressures in forcing the King to restore multi-party constitution and hand over power to them. The Nepali Congress leader, Koirala said in his many public meetings that "the time has come for the King to choose between "constitutional monarchy within multi-party set-up or republican setup under the current circumstances".[85] The dilemma of the political parties lies in their neglect by the King and their fear of the Maoists who have a formidable armed strength and do not have faith in parliamentary and democratic institutions. The Maoists, on their own, are also keeping their agitational mode in tact to maintain pressure on the King. This is evident since the first half of April 2003, when student agitation flared up on the question of death of a Maoist sympathizer student-leader in Butwal in police firing. The firing was resorted to disperse students protest demonstrations on economic demands of rise in the prices of petroleum products, etc.[86] The students are also

85 *Kathmandu Post*, 7 April 2003.
86 *The Kathmandu Post*, 11, 12 and 13 April 2003.

agitating on the question of elections in the University. This agitation continues and it threatens to have country-wide strikes on 27, 28 April.

The international community also does not seem to be very responsive to the Maoists. The US and UK have refused to meet the Maoist representatives. Justifying his negative response to the Maoists, the US Ambassador in Kathmandu Malinowski said: "Given their violent history of destroying infrastructure projects, does any one take the Maoists seriously".[87] The British Ambassador has avoided meeting the Maoists by forwarding their request to London for instructions, but he has stated in Kathmandu that the root causes of the Maoists' uprising will have to be addressed seriously.[88] The EU Representative has met the Maoists but Indian and Chinese representatives in Kathmandu are still to be approached. The Indian Ambassador in Kathmandu has come out with a statement saying that if the Maoists are willing to function democratically then they will not be treated as terrorists. It may, however, be noted here that the general public opinion thinks that the Maoists are serious in their peace talks this time than on the earlier occasion in August 2001. The Maoists' Central Committee's decision, in its first statement on ceasefire and talks in February 2003 (19 *Magh 2059*, Nepali calendar) to involve intellectuals and eminent public figures as facilitators in the talks with the King, was also an indication of their seriousness.

---

87 *The Himalayan Times*, (Kathmandu), 3 April 2003.
88 <nepalnews.com> 16 April 2003.

The third possibility is that the King and the Maoists may strike a deal, leaving the political parties on the fringe.[89] The basis of a deal between these two fundamentally conflicting groups lie in the fact that the King is willing to talk to them, even accommodate some of their critical demands such as the release of their leaders and not recognising them as terrorists. The King has also invoked the concept of 'patriotism' in his addresses to underline a possible common point between him and the Maoists. The Maoists have dropped their demand of a republican State and are willing to adjust with a monarchy with reduced role in any new future set-up. They have also indicated their willingness to give up the demand of Constituent Assembly, since considerable reservations on this demand have been expressed by the political parties. We have earlier noted that the Maoists have often shown the resilience on their stated demands in order to achieve their desired goal of getting closer to power. Underlining the flexibility in their approach in the forthcoming negotiations, Baburam Bhattarai said recently:

The current politics is a conflict between two regimes and three political forces. For the strategic balance no party side can lead the country alone. As such we are advocating for a progressive solution. The major

---

89 For views expressed in Nepal to this effect see "Maoists need to clarify certain pertinent questions", in *The Telegraph, (Weekly)*, Kathmandu 2 April 2003. Also Ram. S. Mahat, "Government – Maoist meeting of minds", *The Kathmandu Post*, 10 April 2003.

agenda of the talks is for all the three forces — pro-monarchist, parliamentary parties and us — to come out with a solution from give and take. The new system would not be like Panchayat or the current parliamentary system. How far we will achieve it depends on the negotiation.... Every one has to show certain flexibility. The bottom line should be the interest of the general public.[90]

The Maoists and the King also had some rapport and understanding between them during King Birendra's regime. They have also come to accept the continuing role of monarchy, but without any effective power or any guarantee for hereditary rule of succession. That is why the Maoists leader Baburam Bhattarai has proposed Cambodian King Sihanouk like status for the Nepali monarch in a new political order.[91] It may be extremely difficult for the King to accept such a status, particularly for a power conscious and ambitious King like Gyanendra, unless forced beyond his capacity. The monarchy's mind-set, since the coming to power of King Mahendra in 1955, is such that it may not accept a truncated status, shorn of any residual or potential power for itself. The King may also not be willing to risk the future of his family by accepting the Cambodian model. The basic positions of the King and the Maoists are such that for any deal between them substantial compromises

90 Interview given to Prateek Pradhan and Guna Raj Luitel, *The Kathmandu Post*, 2 April 2003.

91 Keshav Pradhan, "Nepal Maoists offer Sihanouk-like role to monarch", *The Hindustan Times* (New Delhi), 13 April 2003.

will have to be made by both the sides. Their common interest lies in keeping the political parties marginalized. No wonder then, the King has not involved the parties in the process of negotiations. The only accommodation gestured to the political parties in this respect is by the Deputy Prime Minister and the head of the King's negotiating team, to ask political parties if they want to join the Committee proposed to be set-up to give direction to the negotiating team. The parties have rejected this offer. The Maoists are also not asking for or insisting on the political parties' presence on the negotiating table. All they keep repeating is that the political parties and other political and civil society representatives should be involved in the proposed 'Round Table' discussions that no one know when will be launched, if at all.

Though it is not stated clearly, even the King and the Maoists also share their views of Nepal's relations with India where the former should have greater degree of freedom and autonomy in dealing with the latter. The Maoists would also like to see the reduced US influence in the kingdom that may not be compatible with the king's preferences. Thus in totality, a deal between the king and the Maoists may also be easier said than done, but possibility exists. The political parties are weak and directionless at the moment but they have the potential to vitiate any such deal worked out between the King and the Maoists. Similarly, India will also not let its stakes eroded in Nepal. The US has already made it clear that they would not allow the Maoists to prevail even in a negotiated resolution of the problem.

Of the three possible scenarios, Nepal cannot afford to see itself plunged into violence and anarchy once again. The economic and social costs of the collapse of negotiations and resumption of hostilities will be enormous. This is some thing that no one should allow to happen. In fact, the international community, including the donor group and multilateral financial institutions, are offering substantial economic incentives to encourage the combatants to work for a resolution of the conflict. The best course will be the evolution of a package of political reforms in Nepal that accommodates constructive concerns of all the three principal forces in Nepal, viz., the Maoists, the king and the political parties. One can only wish and hope that this happens.

Origin and Development of the Communist Party of Nepal (Maoist)

Key to Chart Overleaf

ULF: United Left Fronts
1. NL=Nirmal Lama NCP Fourth Convention
2. Rohit=Narayan Man Bijkchhe Nepal Workers and Peasant' Party
3. V=Krishna Das Verma, NCP
4. A=Tulsi Lal Amatya, NCP
5. M=Bishnu Bahadur Manandhan NCP
6. MX=NCP Marxist, Sahana Pradhan
7. ML=NCP Marxist & Leninist
8. Ind=Independent (Padma Ratna Tuladhar)

UPNM: United National People's Movement
1. MB=Mohan Bikram Singh, NCP-Masal
2. PR=Prachanda-Pushpa Kamat Dahal, NCP Mashal
3. RL=Rup Lat Bishworkarma, NCP-People Oriented
4. SR=Shambhu Ram Shrestha, NCP League
5. KD=Krishna Das Shrestha, NCP-Marxist Leninist Maoists.

Bidari=NCP-People Oriented (Ramnarayan Bidan-rebelled from Ruper Bista)

* BB=Baburam Bhattarat joined Unity Centre informally for functional before leaving his party-Masal. Actually he was in position for party or Due to this reason he left his party and joined Unity Centre

UPFN (Vaidya)=Niranjan Gevinda Vaidya

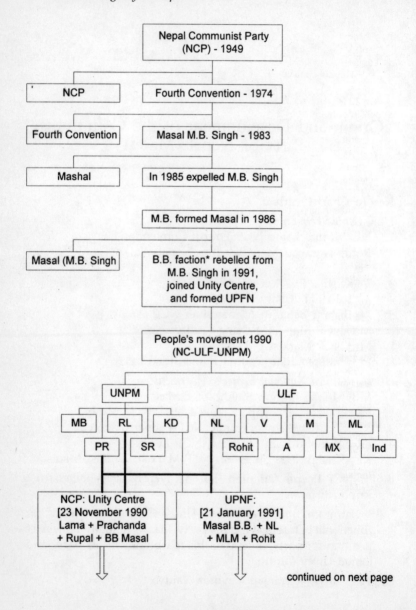

continued on next page

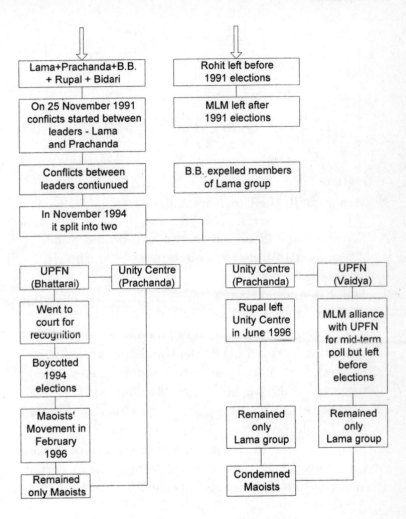

Annexure II

40-Point Demand of the Maoists

1 Demands Related to Nationalism

1. Regarding the 1950 Treaty between India and Nepal, all unequal stipulations and agreements should be removed.
2. HMG should admit that the anti-nationalist Tanakpur agreement was wrong, and the Mahakali Treaty, incorporating it, should be nullified.
3. The entire Nepal–India border should be controlled and systematized. Cars with Indian numberplates, plying the roads of Nepal, should not be allowed.
4. Gorkha recruiting centres should be closed and decent jobs should be arranged for the recruits.
5. In several areas of Nepal, where foreign technicians are given precedence over Nepalese technicians for certain jobs, a system of work permits should be instituted for the foreigners.
6. The monopoly of foreign capital in Nepal's industry, trade and economic sector should be stopped.
7. Sufficient income should be generated from customs duties for the country's economic development.

8. The cultural pollution of imperialists and expansionists should be stopped. Hindi video, cinema, and all kinds of such newspapers and magazines should be completely stopped. Inside Nepal, import and distribution of Vulgar Hindi films, video cassettes and magazines should be stopped.

9. Regarding NGOs and INGOs. Bribing by imperialists and expansionists in the name of NGOs and INGOs should be stopped.

2 Demands Related to the Public Welfare

10. A new Constitution has to be drafted by the people's elected representatives.

11. All the special rights and privileges of the King and his family should be ended.

12. Army, police and administration should be under the people's control.

13. The Security Act and all other repressive acts should be abolished.

14. All the false charges against the people of Rukum, Rolpa, Jajrkot, Gorkha, Kavre, Sindhuphalchowk, Sindhuli, Dhanusha and Remechap should be withdrawn and all the people falsely charged should be released.

15. Armed police operations in the different districts should immediately be stopped.

16. Regarding Dilip Chaudhary, Bhuvan Thapa Magar, Prabhakar Subedi and other people who disappeared from police custody at different times, the government should constitute a special investigating committee to

look into these crimes and the culprits should be punished and appropriate compensation given to their families.

17. People, who died during the time of the movement, should be declared as martyrs and their families, and those who have been wounded and disabled should be given proper compensation. Strong action should be taken against the killers.

18. Nepal should be declared a secular state.

19. Girls should be given equal property rights to those of their brothers.

20. All kinds of exploitation and prejudice based on caste should be ended. In areas having a majority of one ethnic group, that group should have autonomy over that area.

21. The status of dalits as untouchables should be ended and the system of untouchability should be ended once and for all.

22. All languages should be given equal status. Up until middle-high school level (uccha-madyamic) arrangements should be made for education to be given in the children's mother tongue.

23. There should be guarantee of free speech and free Press. The communications media should be completely autonomous.

24. Intellectuals, historians, artists and academicians engaged in other cultural activities should be guaranteed intellectual freedom.

25. In both the tarai and hilly regions there is prejudice and misunderstanding in backward areas. This should be

ended and the backward areas should be assisted. Good relations should be established between the villages and the city.

26. Decntralization in real terms should be applied to local areas which should have local rights, autonomy and control over their own resources.

3 Demands Related to the People's Living

27. Those who cultivate the land should own it. (The tiller would have right to the soil he/she tills.) The land of rich landlords should be confiscated and distributed to the homeless and others who have no land.

28. Brokers and commission agents should have their property confiscated and that money should be invested in industry.

29. All should be guaranteed work and should be given stipend until jobs are found for them.

30. HMG should pass strong laws ensuring that people involved in industry and agriculture should receive minimum wages.

31. The homeless should be given suitable accommodation. Until HMG can provide such accommodation they should not be removed from where they are squatting.

32. Poor farmers should be completely freed from debt. Loans from the Agricultural Development Bank by poor farmers should be completely written off. Small industries should be given loans.

33. Fertilizer and seeds should be easily and cheaply available, and the farmers should be given a proper market price for their production.

34. Flood and drought victims should be given all necessary help.
35. All should be given free and scientific medical service and education and education for profit (private schools?) should be completely stopped.
36. Inflation should be controlled and labourers' salaries should be raised in direct ratio with the rise in prices. Daily essential goods should be made cheap and easily available.
37. Arrangement should be made for drinking water, good roads, and electricity in the villages.
38. Cottage and other small industries should be granted special facilities and protection.
39. Corruption, black marketeering, smuggling, bribing, the taking of commission, etc., should all be stopped.
40. Orphans, the disabled, the elderly and children should be given help and protection.

We offer a heartfelt request to the present coalition government that they should, fulfil the above demands which are essential for Nepal's existence and for the people's daily lives as soon as possible. If the government does not show any interest by 5 Falgun 2052,17 (February 1996) we will be compelled to launch a movement against the government. The above demands put forth by the Samyukta Jana Morcha, led by Dr Bhattarai, were handed over to the then prime minister Sher Bahadur Deuba.

The government showed no interest in fulfilling any of the above demands, or even taking these seriously. After a cruel government crackdown on members of the Samyukta

Jana Morcha (which previously held nine seats in the parliament), in Rukum, and Rolpa, Dr Bhattarai declared the 'Jana Yudha.'

Source: Pancha N. Maharjan, "The Maoist Insurgency and Crisis of Governability in Nepal", in Dhruba Kumar (Ed.) *Domestic Conflict and Crisis of Governability in Nepal.*

CNAS, Centre for Nepal and Asian Studies
Tribhuvan University, Kathmandu 2000
Pages 191-193

Annexure — III

Major Maoist Operations in Nepal during November 2001 to December 2002

S. No.	Date	Place/Region	Target	Enemy Force	Result
1	23-Nov-01	Ghorahi/West	Dist. HQ**	RNA+AFP+PF	Total Success
2	23-Nov-01	Syangja/West	Dist. HQ**	AFP+PF	Total Success
3	25-Nov-01	Salleri/East	Dist. HQ**	RNA+AFP+PF	Success except RNA
4	07-Dec-01	Ratmate/West	Telecom Security Camp	RNA	Failure
5	08-Dec-01	Kapurkot/West	Telecom Security Camp	RNA	Failure
6	05-Feb-02	Bhakundebeshi/East	APO	AFP+PF	Total Success
7	16-Feb-02	Mangalsen/West	Dist. HQ**	RNA+AFP+PF	Total Success
8	16-Feb-02	Sanfebagar/West	Airport	AFP+PF	Total Success
9	16-Feb-02	Lalbandi/East	APO	AFP+PF	Total Success
10	11-Apr-02	Satbaria/West	APF Camp	AFP	Total Success

S. No.	Date	Place/Region	Target	Enemy Force	Result
11	11-Apr-02	Lamahi/West	APO	PF	Total Success
12	17-Apr-02	Barpak/Centre	APO	AFP+PF	Total Success
13	02-May-02	Lisne/West	RNA Base Camp	RNA Company	Total Success
14	07-May-02	Gam/West	RNA Camp	RNA (Company)	Total Success
15	07-May-02	Chainpur/East	Dist. Sub HQ**	RNA	Failure
16	27-May-02	Khara/West	RNA Camp	RNA	Failure
17	30-May-02	Damachaur/West	RNA Base Camp	RNA	Success
18	08-Sep-02	Bhiman/East	APO	AFP+PF	Total Success
19	10-Sep-02	Sandhikharka/West	Dist. HQ**	RNA+AFP+PF	Total Success
20	27-Oct-02	Rumjatar/East	Airport	RNA	Failure
21	14-Nov-02	Jumla/West	Zonal HQ*	RNA+AFP+PF	Success except RNA
22	14-Nov-02	Takukot/Centre	APO	AFP+PF	Total Success
23	04-Dec-02	Lahan/East	APO+Bank	AFP+PF	Total Success

Note: RNA = Royal Nepal Army; APF = Armed Police Force; PF = Ordinary Police Force; APO = Area Police Office; Dist. HQ = District Headquarters.

* Zonal HQ has Batallion level of RNA formation plus other forces.
** District HQ has Company Level of RNA formation plus other forces.
* Others generally have platoon level of security forces.

Source: *The Worker.* Organ of the CPN (Maoist); No: 8 January 2003

United Revolutionary People's Council

Nepal's Minimum United Policy and Program

Nepal's minimum united policy and program has been concluded to usher in the direction of united struggle and the rule achieving therefrom, in process of new revolution or people's revolution. An effort shall be made to invariably enforce such policies in the areas, where the local level people's rule has already formed. They shall also be practised in other areas and the central level mainly with the purpose of publicity and revolution.

Chapter 1 — Fundamental Policies

1. The principal purpose of the new people's congress is to institutionalize the people's congress and people's republic rule in the nation. Likewise, the fundamental features of new people's republic rule is to end all forms of exploitation of national capitalist and imperialist/expansionist in the leadership labour and peasant unity and to enforce the dominance of people's rule over the enemies.

2. The new people's rule can only be established in nation if the movement is towered ahead with establishing base area in the local areas of village and route of strategic and long-term war is followed. Likewise, it seems essential to go ahead with the inclusion of the notable points of the armed revolt in people's war that has begun in the specific geo-historical condition of Nepal and present world scenario. The people's congress shall thus unite and mobilize rival powers — the feudal and imperialists/expansionists to reach the people's war to the winning point through the implementation of specific troops strategies.

3. In the new people's rule, the absolute sovereignty shall be vested in the people. The guarantee of which shall be given by forming the new Constitution constituted by the representatives elected through adult franchise in the initiative of an interim government formed with the participation of all rival feudal imperialists and expansionists after the downfall of existing reactionary rule by people's war.

4. There shall be a guarantee of all fundamental and political rights of the people like the right to speech and expression, to elect and be elected, and to own or disown the religion end to live in the places liked. Employment, education and health shall be guaranteed as the fundamental rights of people. In the new people's rule, there shall be guarantee of full freedom with the help that the various patriotists and that it obtains from communist parties. It is against the rumour of the reactionists, which follows people's communists party

is a despotic rule. The reactionists, who played the role of counter-revolutionists and act against the interest of nation and people, shall be deprived of all political rights for a certain period. Along with the exercise of fundamental rights, all the citizens shall abide by their own duties of protection of nation, follow Constitution and Law, protection of the public property and compliance of labour discipline, providing military service and paying taxes.

5. There shall not be discrimination among any persons on the ground of class, race, religion, sex, area, and state shall treat all people equally and provide an equal guarantee of opportunity. Equal wage shall be ascertained with equal work to all.

6. State shall be made separate from religion and a secular state shall be established exclusively and there shall not be discrimination among the various religions. All types of cheating, corruption, exploitation and violence happening in the name of religion shall be prohibited.

7. The nation shall entirely be made sovereign, independent, self-dependent by ending all semi-colonial and new-colonial agreements including the treaty of 1950 and freeing the nation from loan shouldered on the nation by the imperialists and expansionists. All citizens shall be provided the employment opportunity within nation by closing the Gorkha Recruitment Centre running as the national college. The rampant exploitation of imperialists over the water resource shall be ended and it shall be used in the common interest of people.

8. All the feudal bureaucratic, capitalists and expansionists linkages existing in national economy shall be ended and national capitalistic linkage shall be developed. Socialism induced capitalistic linkages shall be maintained in economy by not implementing socialists linkages in beforehand. There shall be maintained an appropriate balance between private, united and joint ownership or the collective ownership of the state over the mega and prioritized industries. And, financial institution and of farmers over the agro-based industries and private sector over them which are small, medium scale industries and enterprises. No nationalization of an individual property shall be made except in accordance with law. To transform the backwardness of extremely deprived producer, the main economic policy shall be applied with the vision "catch the revolution up strongly and increase the production".

9. The fundamental principle of the state shall be the people's centrality. And the consideration shall be given to maintain a balance between the people's rule and centrality. The state shall guarantee the right to open discussion among people, free speech, placing a big poster in the place and provide protection to the people's rule based right, and the right to strike belonging to labour shall be protected.

Chapter 2 — State System

10. The state power shall entirely be vested with people. Different level different representative and assembly and

people's committee shall be the organs of state rule. All levels' representatives shall be elected on the basis of adult franchise through election. The people's representative assembly shall elect the people's committee government of concerned level. The people's committees shall rule as the main organs when there is no meeting of the people's assembly to sit.

11. The people's assembly and people's committee's government shall be formed in four tiers like the central level, autonomous region, autonomous district, village/municipal level. In the context of specific war, there shall always be board people's committee under the village level board. And, they shall have to work under the village people's representative or people's committee. In the areas where the ethnic unity exists, people's representative and people's government will work.

12. The people's assembly shall be the most superior with the legislative and executive power, nor the bourgeois parliament. They shall be representative of all groups, castes, people of all areas and representative of people's military, and they shall guarantee themselves as the real people's rule as they are to be patriots and the specific representatives of people's cadres. They shall be responsible towards people as the people deserve the power of recall to their representative when they are dissatisfied with their representatives' work.

13. The National Conference of People's Congress shall exercise the power of national people's assembly until the appropriate situation for holding election of

revolutionary united front machinery happens, as its election is to be held based on adult franchise and in which the powers like people's assembly, labour, peasant, people's military, lower capitalists, national level capitalist, ethnic communities, women and immigrants are to be represented. Therefore, the national people's representative shall pass the constitution and rules, elect the national government, and authorize for the state rule.

14. The military and non-military representatives shall be deployed for electing the local level government by central government in the areas where it seems impossible to hold election of different level representative due to the collapse of the institution during war. The local level government shall be formed by the all-parties representatives assembly. An election shall be held after the appropriate situation prepares.

15. Different level people's representatives and people's committee shall come into existence and operation in accordance with the principles of centrality of people's representatives' assembly, people's committee and people's government whereby the people's representatives shall be responsible towards people. The minority has to accept the rule of majority with the people's assembly and people's government and various kinds of appointments shall be ratified by the upper level organ and it shall have to follow the decision reached at by the upper level organ. In all the places, the decision of the central government shall be followed and consent shall be reached at in the case of the autonomous organs.

16. The powers and jurisdiction of the central and local level people's government shall be defined and the central government shall issue the appropriate order keeping in view the national unity and local utility.

17. All the laws, orders and judicial systems of the old reactionary rule shall be repealed and terminated. In the interest of the people, new laws and orders shall come into force and people's rule based judicial system will be established.

18. To render into justice, various tiers of people's court shall be constituted of which officials shall be appointed by the people's assembly and be responsible towards it.

19. The machinery handling security shall exercise the powers relating to sue the case as a prosecutor, of the level concerned. While suing a case against anybody, the people's direction shall appropriately be used and the community shall itself be participated in the pleading of the criminal cases sued against the main reactionaries.

20. An honest, simple and the revolutionary working system shall be applied in all organs of the nation at all levels and strong opposite voices need to raise against those who are found in corruption, extravagant work and red tapism.

21. The separate organ for the supervision formed by the people shall be established with a view to keep prompt surveillance of the work committed by representatives residing in different levels of people's government. The people shall be empowered to file a case against such

representative in the judicial bodies or supervising bodies constituted.

Chapter 3 — People's Military and People's Security System

22. A united people's military force shall be formed with the participation of the main force, subsidiary local force and militia to dismantle the old reactionaries' rule and to keep the people's rule safe. The supreme commander of the people's military shall be the president of the central committee of communist party. Such body shall be mobilized through the central level people's government. The main rule and the subsidiary rule shall be mobilized centrally and the locally respectively whereas the people's militia provide the local safety.

23. It shall highly be important to unite the people's military to fight with centralized military power of the present imperial rule. To end the bureaucratic culture, as developed in the present reactionary's military, the people's military shall always be guided by the command of revolutionary command. And, people shall be united and a policy to maintain a high relation between military and officer level within people's military shall be followed. To be safe from the danger caused by the reactionary, the whole community shall be militarized with the policy measures and the people's militia shall extensively extended for it.

24. The fundamental work of the people's army is to constantly wage the people's war before the revolution results and to protect the motherland and new rule.

But, it shall work as the producer and consolidator among people during the period it is in leisure.

25. The people shall specifically be motivated for their recruitment in the people's military during revolution and a specific priority shall be given to the injured and handicapped martyrs than their dependent families. The people's government shall pay its proper attention to collect the means and resources needed and special priority shall be given to the military and policy who want to join people's military leaving the camp of reactionary's rule.

Chapter 4 — Agriculture and Land Reformation

26. The agriculture revolution is the fundamental basis of the people's revolution. The main purpose of the agriculture policy is to end the feudal, semi-feudal and bureaucratic production linkages and to develop the national capitalistic linkages of which the essential basis shall be the cultivation of land or the land shall be distributed to the landless and the poor farmers, which is located at the places where the rule of the feudal, bureaucrats and land owned by trustee. And, the peasants shall be given the ownership of such land. No expropriation of the land belonging to rich people and the semi-farmers shall be made. But land ceiling shall be determined and enforced considering the availability of land and the number of the population.

Only the reformative steps shall be implemented in the areas where the old rule has not entirely collapsed.

The land ceiling system shall be maintained and tenant's rights shall be preserved, and rate of land revenue shall be decreased with its division into three folds and the interest shall be deduced and the trust land shall be conserved into registered land.

27. The landless and poor farmers shall perfectly be made free from all sorts of loans and all the labour services and taxes imposed on them shall be repealed.

28. The system of force labour and other exploitation based on feudal rule shall be eliminated and they shall be resettled and provided the opportunity of employment.

29. A minimum wage for the agricultural labour shall be fixed and it shall strongly be enforced. An equal remuneration shall be given to both men and women equally.

30. The agriculture loan shall be provided with the minimum interest rates and in a convenient way. An appropriate provision for the irrigation shall be managed in the cultivable land. Rural infrastructure shall be developed by utilizing the surplus labour force existing in agriculture.

31. The fertilizer, seeds and other agricultural equipment shall be provided in cheap and an expeditious way. A special attention shall be given for the development of agriculture. And, the agriculture market shall be considerably managed. A balance shall be maintained in the price of the agricultural and industrial production.

32. The help of the local level revolutionary peasants shall be obtained to determine the character of landless, poor, semi-feudal and feudal, to prepare the actual record of

the land, and to mobilize the community as a whole. Besides, the land reformation program shall be implemented in phase-wise in the central and regional level and maximum priority shall be given to local experts. A consideration shall be given to enforce the land reformation program to stop chronological encroachment in disadvantaged people's land and on autonomous areas.

33. The land shall be expropriated from the feudal and capitalist bureaucrats and the land if seized from rich farmers and uncultivated pasture land shall be distributed to the local farmers without any discrimination. And such land will be their own private land. In that process, naturally, an evaluation of the quality of the land shall be rationally made based on the category of it.

34. The chattels, agricultural goods, houses and other property expropriated from feudal shall be distributed to poor people and other farmers and it shall be their own private property.

35. The vast forest, irrigation project, mines, pasture land, lakes, river, etc. shall be under the ownership of people's government. Likewise, the historical and the places having the tourism importance and monuments shall be under the people's government.

36. The land shall be distributed equally to the representatives of people's government as it is distributed to other peasants. A special priority shall be given to the family of martyrs in the distribution process. The property and land shall be given to the old feudal and their families

and representative of old rulers for their survival with own labour. But, the property and land shall be distributed to the family member and those who are not involved in the criminal activities on an equal basis.

37. All the documents pertaining to the land loan, ownership and transaction shall be declared null and void existing before the land reformation comes into force and the people's government shall issue new documents to all with a scrutiny process. They shall be punished by the people's court who oppose the land reformation program and violate the rule concerned.

38. The co-operatives shall be promoted to increase the production, for the maximum utilization of labour and increment of the economic growth, as there is small portion of land exists in the hilly area and the production capacity exists at minimum level. A policy to develop the co-operative from smaller to bigger and lower to higher level shall be followed.

39. Considering the diversity exists in mountain, hill and terai and the potentials for the production of different specialties like herbal medicine, horticultural goods, forest product and crops, a policy for the united, balanced and interdependent development shall be followed. A special emphasis shall be given to fulfil the necessity of foodstuff in the war period and afterwards.

Chapter 5 — Industry, Finance and Infrastructure Development

40. There is no possibility of national economic transformation without rapid national industrial development

and fulfilment of prosperous physical and cultural necessity in Nepal as it is badly plugged into extreme poverty, unemployment, semi-unemployment, undeveloped and dependent situation. Therefore, the way of industrialization shall be taken ahead with the nationalization of the property of bureaucratic capitalists and brokers on the one hand, and on the other freeing the national industries from the shackles of Indian monopoly for achieving the rapid economic development. Moreover, the cottage, small and the marginal industrialists shall be promoted and their property be protected along with the industrialization.

41. The industries using local raw material and skill and supplying these goods, in the base areas, like clothes, shoes, equipment and paper shall be given high emphasis during the war. A special priority shall be given to the import substitution industries keeping in view the probable economic blockade that can be caused by the imperialists and expansionists during war and afterwards.

42. The labour-induced industrialization shall mainly be emphasised realizing the condition of the shortage of capital and abundance of labour exists for a long time in nation. A special attention shall be given to fulfil the industrial energy and guarantee the sustainable development by the small hydropower projects with the utilization of available large manpower.

A strategic effort shall be made for the balanced development of rural, urban, and hilly and terai agriculture, and industry, small, large and modern industry by ending existing economic and geographical inequality.

43. A mininum wage system and provision for 40 working hours shall be fixed for labourers and it shall be strongly implemented. There shall be given guarantee for the participation of labourers in the management of industries. The co-operative system shall be emphasized on the cottage and small-scale industries.

44. The trade of basic goods and foreign trade shall be in the hand of state whereas other sector's trade shall be in the hand of private sector. The Indians' monopoly shall be ended that exists in the trade sector so far. The national trader shall be protected by the state and commercial relation shall be maintained based on mutual loss and gain.

45. The consumer co-operatives shall be prioritized in supply of consumed goods in cheap price and fair way. To maintain the price stability, the nation will interfere as per necessity. Required custom policy shall be followed to give a protection to the domestic products. A special provision shall be made to make available of the goods needed in the remote areas.

46. The exploitation and sufferings existing within the nation shall be ended and nation shall be made free from foreign loan. The financial institution shall be made free to do transaction in rural areas to provide loan there. But, the interest rate shall be controlled.

47. The public expenditure shall be managed under the budget system. The tax policy shall be formed keeping in view the need of war and economic rehabilitation.

48. The imperialists' financial intervention caused by NGOs and INGOs shall be ended.

49. The communication and transportation system shall be planned considering the hardships of hilly region. A consideration shall be given to construct the road, bridge, highways and other physical infrastructure in rural areas. The planned urbanization shall be developed from the unplanned one. The planned settlement system shall be considered in newly immuned areas.

50. The small scale hydro project shall be emphasized as against the mega ones. The development of tourism shall be made in favour of common people.

Chapter 6 — Culture and Education

51. The main character of new people's culture and education shall be people-oriented and scientific one. The main task of people in the area of culture and education shall be to increase cultural development and to serve the nation and to achieve the progressive and scientific opinion. The new people's education and culture shall create a sense of curiosity of people in people's dignity, homage towards science and labour.

52. The education shall be made free, compulsory and fair. The adult and literacy programs shall be ended with the movement of special literacy. Maintaining a balance between natural science and social science shall provide the education. A special priority shall be given to the polytechnic education. Due consideration shall be given to higher education and technical education.

53. Repealing the earlier shall scientifically make the new curriculum. All shall be provided the education in own mother language.
54. A special consideration shall be given for the preservation and development of culture and art. The art and literature that increases the social and political awareness shall be given priority. The priority shall be given to people's military and people's forum for dancing. The best literatures of art shall be awarded prize. A ban shall be made on vulgar literature and films.
55. The right to speech and expression of the people shall be protected. A motivation shall be created for publishing factual newpapers. The radio and publication program shall be promoted. An emphasis shall be given to the publication of the popular and useful books.
56. The old cultural monuments shall be protected. A special emphasis shall be given to the language and culture of the disadvantaged groups.

Chapter-7—Health and Social Welfare

57. The health facility shall be provided to all freely. The health sector's development shall be emphasized in rural areas. The modern health service shall be practised by ending the old Dhadi Ghakries. A special emphasis shall be given in the production of lower and middle level trained health manpower. Some existing system developed by imperialists concerned with the import of many harmful medicines shall be ended and the promotion of herbal medicine shall be made.

58. The right of the disabled, old people and disadvantaged shall be protected and they shall be given due care.
59. All shall be provided a minimum guarantee of settlement facilities. Due provision shall be made for homeless people.

Chapter 8 — Question relating to caste and region

60. An equal treatment shall be made to all castes and languages that exist within nation. All the Aryan rural and other marginalized may exercise their rights derived by the tradition and custom. But, their problems arising out of the new rule shall be settled in accordance with autonomous program. According to which, all sorts of imposition over the marginalized shall be ended. They shall be empowered to rule within their area autonomously. There can be more than one autonomous rule where there exists more than one caste. The people's government elected by them shall be the main tools of their rule. The autonomous rule shall have an exclusive rule over all except over the matter of people's military, foreign relation, finance, communication, international trade and basic industries, etc. They shall have power to rule autonomously within the laws and rules passed.
61. There shall be proportional representation of each caste within an autonomous area if other castes reside there also.
62. All the marginalized castes shall have a right to be recruited in people's military. And, militia shall be formed under the command of centre for the local security.

63. All marginalized castes shall have full freedom to develop own languages and to practise the traditional norms, etc. The central government shall help them in the making of the policy concerning with political, economic, cultural and education sector.

64. The local level autonomous rule shall be formed in high mountainous region, Karnali, Seti and Mahakali areas which are facing the disparity due to imbalance in economic development. The form of the regional autonomous rule shall be similar to the form of caste based autonomous rule.

65. The question of terai is the question of ethnic and regional disparity where many castes live. However, the main question is of ethnic disparity. The separate autonomous areas shall be formed in terai where different languages like Maithali, Bhojpuri, Abadhi are spoken and different ethnic groups live. All types of discrimination in terai region shall be ended. The long pending problem of citizenship in terai region shall be solved in a scientific, judicious way.

Chapter 9 — Women and Family

66. All types of patriarchal exploitation over the women shall be ended. And, women shall be given equal right to the man in all areas. An equal ancestral property right shall be given to daughter as the son. Women shall be given privilege in all level government machineries for their participation. All sorts of prostitution including badi, jhuma and the social evils shall entirely be ended.

Offender of women trafficking shall be strictly punished. The sold Nepalese women within the nation and outside it shall be rehabilitated with dignity by freeing them from that profession.

67. No marriage between man and woman can be solemnized by coercion and other tradition without free will. There shall have to be united in marriage. The minimum age of male 22 and female 20 should be there for marrying. The marriage shall be registered before the representative of people's government after an inquiry is made over. It shall be the duty of couple to maintain a small family, to go for family planning. The right to abortion of women shall be protected. Widow marriage shall be prioritized. Child care shall be given due consideration.

68. A divorce can be possible in the interest of both husband and wife. The power to decide the case shall be upon the people's government if a party puts his/her interest off. The issue of women shall be given priority in the cases in which women have been exploited. The father and mother's duty to bear the cost of feeding their child will be in ratio of 2/3 and 1/3, respectively.

Chapter 10 — Downtrodden Castes

69. All forms of exploitations and disparities over the downtrodden castes based on Hindu caste system shall be ended and they shall be equal to other castes in all respects. A strict criminal proceeding shall be processed against him/her who treats other with untouchabiltity.

70. State shall provide special protection to untouchables and disadvantaged groups who are economically and socially backward until they obtain equal rights to other castes and such rights shall be enforced with rules.

Chapter 11 — Foreign Policy

71. It shall be tried to maintain the friendly relation with all nations over the world, in accordance with the principles of panchshil like the sovereignty, national integrity, non-intervention and equal and mutual co-existence.
72. The main basis of the foreign policy of people's republic of Nepal shall be to preserve the nation's freedom and sovereignty and to keep safe the people's system, and to promote the imperialists and expansionists.
73. All the agreements/treaties which are not in the interest of nation and concluded by the old rule, they shall be renewed by their inquiry made over by the new people's rule.
74. A strong relation shall be extended with different revolutionary groups and national freedom movements that are fighting against the Indian expansionist, the main external enemy within South Asia. And, an effort shall be made to form a South Asian soviet federation with revolution in all countries.
75. The interest of Nepalese residing in foreign country, mainly in India shall be protected. An appropriate provision shall be made for the Nepalese people who have left their nation in search of employment, providing

them the employment in nation. A special attention shall be given to the problem of brain drain and to use their resources and skills. The foreigners shall be given a protection by the state who reside in Nepal according to Nepalese law. Political asylum shall be given to the citizens of any foreign nation who were compelled to leave their nation due to their involvement in revolutionary activities if they live in Nepal bound by Nepalese law.

The above unauthentic English translation was obtained through sources in Nepal. This programme was adopted at the first national conference of the United Revolutionary Peoples' Council of the Maoists held in Western Nepal in September 2001. A copy of this programme in Nepali was presented by the Maoist leader Dr Baburam Bhattarai in his interaction with the Federation of Nepal Chamber of Commerce and Industry in March 2003. The original Nepali version may be found in the Maoist magazine *Tesro Sansar* (Third World – Committed to the Oppressed Nations and People) Yr 2, No 2, 30 May 2002, pp 11–16.

Annexure — V

From cease-fire to first round of peace talks 2003

By Guna Raj Luitel,
Assistant Editor, *Kantipur Daily*,
Kathmandu, Nepal

January 29
- Government-Maoist declares cease-fire.
- Previous government's decision of declaring Maoist terrorists revoked.
- Government to notify INTERPOL to Withdraw red corner notice issued against Maoist leaders.
- Previous government's decision of fixing price tag on heads of Maoist leaders withdrawn.
- Maoist still adamant on round-table conference, interim government and election to constituent assembly.

January 30
- News of cease-fire thrills kith and kin of Maoist top brass. International community lauds truce.
- UK's Foreign Office Minister Mike O'Brien welcomed the important and positive development.

– India said, "the process of dialogue should be based on national consensus, should involve political parties and should be conducted in an environment free from violence ... we continue to regard multi-party democracy and constitutional monarchy as the two pillars for stability in Nepal."
– European Head of Mission says, "this encouraging development will bring a durable cessation of hostilities, intimidation and destruction that have caused so much suffering to the people of Nepal."
– Embassy of Finland, which is carrying the duties of the EU Presidency, emphasized that "the forthcoming negotiation should be a starting point to a political process leading to the integration of the Maoists into the mainstream of the political life in Nepal and to the creation of the right condition for free and fair elections."
– The US Embassy has also welcomed the immediate cessation of all Maoist military activities and terrorist attacks.
– German Ambassador to Nepal, Rudiger Lemp, welcomed the cessation of military activities and hoped that negotiations would become successful.

January 31
– Minister Pun meets jailed Maoist.
– UN Secretary General Kofi Annan said he is "encouraged by these developments."
– China, Japan welcomed truce.
  China — "one significant and positive step towards peace."

"China sincerely hopes all political forces and people of insight in Nepal could work together to resolve the present problems, and realize the peace, stability and development in Nepal at the earliest."

- However, the political parties sing different tunes about peace process
. Nepali Congress president Girija Prasad Koirala is among the top leaders who are positive about playing role in favour of the peace dialogue. Similarly, the Communist Party of Nepal–Unified Marxist and Leninist (CPN–UML) has come out in favour of the constituent assembly, interim government and round table conference if that helps in securing long-term peace and resolution of Maoist problem.
- However, Nepali Congress (Democratic) leader and former Prime Minister Sher Bahadur Deuba ruled out any possibility of his party joining the peace process.

February 1
- Questioning the legitimacy of cease-fire declared on 29 January, the Communist Party of Nepal–Unified Marxist & Leninist (CPN–UML), cautioned Maoist leaders not to bring the king into active politics, as the party's seventh national congress kicked off in Janakpur.
- During a situation when the government-Maoist ceasefire is proceeding towards a peaceful dialogue, Madhav Kumar Nepal, general secretary of UML and Amik Serchan, president of Peoples' Front Nepal on Saturday made public about their talks with one of the Maoist leaders.

February 2
- Dr Baburam Bhattarai, principal ideologue of the underground Maoists, will be heading a five-member team to negotiate with the government. The team members announced by party supremo Pushpa Kamal Dahal a.k.a. Prachanda include Ram Bahadur Thapa a.k.a. Badal, Dev Gurung, Krishna Bahadur Mahara and Matrika Prasad Yadav.
- The Maoists have also announced withdrawal of the two-day nation-wide general strikes (Nepal Bandh) scheduled for 13 and 14 February in order to create a conducive atmosphere for dialogue.

February 5
- Prachanda holds telephonic talks with Narayan Man Bijukchhe, Nepal Worker's and Peasants' Party.

February 9
- Communist Party of Nepal–Unified Marxist & Leninist (CPN–UML) and Nepal Congress have agreed upon calling an all-party meet soon, to discuss the negotiation process.
- RPP leaders warns that Maoists might regroup during truce.

February 10
- Madhav Kumar Nepal. General Secretary of CPN–UML said that there was no need to include the king in the possible Round Table talks with the Maoists to find a way out of the current crises.

- Narayan Singh Pun vetoes re-arrest of freed Maoist. He hold talks with the Maoists, had to rush to Nakkhu Jail today, to pacify about 24 agitating Maoists who were protesting against the re-arrest of one of their colleagues soon after his release.

February 11
- The Maoists had a detailed discussion and understanding with a special emissary of the king before the truce was declared on 29 January. People's Front Nepal (PFN) chief Amik Sherchan said, quoting the Maoist Supremo Prachanda.

February 12
- The four major political parties — UML, NC, NWPP and PFN — appeared moving closer in demanding revival of House of Representatives.

February 12
- CPN-Maoist leader Prachanda has conceded that the cease-fire declaration was a part of a strategic balancing act following government's willingness to concede certain demands of them. "The decision like taking the CPN-Maoist off the terrorist list and annulling the red corner notices against its leaders created atmosphere conducive for declaring cease-fire followed by dialogue," Prachanda said in a statement.

February 14
- The first ever all-party meeting called by Prime Minister Lokendra Bahadur Chand to discuss the peace process is being boycotted by the major political parties.

February 16
- Prachanda orders cadres to halt extortion.
- The official negotiator for the government-Maoist peace talks, Narayan Singh Pun announced that those who have committed atrocities in dealing with the Maoists and ordinary people in exercise of the state authority would be sent to war crime tribunals once the peace talks were over.

February 17
- The first ever all-party meeting called by Prime Minister Lokendra Bahadur Chand to discuss Maoist problem ended in a fiasco as all major political parties, including the Rastriya Prajatantra Party (RPP), boycotted it. Only six parties without representatives in the dissolved Parliament attended the meeting, which lasted for less than an hour.

February 20
- Maoists have today apologized to the parents of two students killed and one seriously injured in a shooting incident at Prabha Secondary School. The two students died and one was injured while the Maoists were instructing them on how to use guns.
- Krishna Bahadur Mahara, a member of the Maoist negotiation team and Dinanath Sharma, a Politburo member of the Maoist party committed to make all pre-ceasefire developments transparent to the political parties and the civic society, during a meeting with the CPN-ML leader C.P. Mainali and by telephone with the CPN-UML leader Bamdev Gautam.

February 21
- Surya Bahadur Thapa, former chairman of the RPP, said just after the meeting two Maoist leaders Krishna Bahadur Mahara and Dinanath Sharma that the Maoist is sincere and serious to solve the problem through dialogue.

February 23
- The Communist Party of Nepal (Maoist) Politburo members Krishna Bahadur Mahara and Dinanath Sharma met former prime minister Kirti Nidhi Bista and told him that they were very positive in bringing about a logical conclusion to the current cease-fire.

February 25
- Prachanda, the Chairman of Maoist, in a telephonic conversation with Girija Prasad Koirala, President of Nepali Congress on Monday night, has urged the latter to co-operate for a political solution to the current problems.

  Army welcomes cease-fire and warns of 'decisive war' if rebels 'betray'.

February 26
- The government is determined to bring the peace talks with Maoists to a logical conclusion with or without political parties' participation in the peace process, Minister Narayan Singh Pun said.

February 27
- Narayan Singh Pun, the co-ordinator of the government side to hold talks with the Maoists. today helf informal talks with Krishna Bahadur Mahara, a member of the

Maoist negotiating team, to finalize the code of conduct for the post ceasefire period.

March 3

- The donor community has shown willingness in extending additional assistance worth millions of rupees for the reconstruction of infrastructure and to resume basic services in areas like education and health, and has urged the government to present a comprehensive development package of implementation.
- Krishna Bahadur Mahara and Dina Nath Sharma, members of the Maoist-negotiation team in separate meetings with the leaders of the UML, NC and NSP, alleged that the government was not fulfilling its part for peaceful dialogue.
- UML has announced month-long nation-wide people's campaign starting 5 March in order to press their demand for all-party government.

March 5

- The Maoist leadership has reacted strongly to a statement issued by a senior US State Department official linking them to the Khmer Rouge guerillas which terrorized Cambodia in the 1970s.
- Law-suit against Maoist leaders.

March 6

- The Maoist leadership has taken strong exception to the filing of the cases against Dr Baburam Bhattarai head of the Maoist negotiating team, and party chairman Prachanda.

March 8
–   In another major disclosure, Narayan Singh Pun said, the government has already procured 1500 tonnes of food grains to feed the Maoist guerillas living in different parts of the country.

March 10
–   His Majesty King Gyanendra reiterated the commitment to the present constitution in separate audiences granted to Nepali Congress (NC) president Girija Prasad Koirala and CPN–UML general secretary Madhav Kumar Nepal, but remained non-committal on the demands raised by both the leaders.
–   All party meeting called by PM is rejected by all major political parties except RPP.

March 11
–   Eleven left parties including the Communist Party of Nepal (Maoist) today agreed to launch a movement against the 4 October royal take over after a joint meeting.
In the first ever meeting with the ten left parties Maoist leader Dinanath Sharma said that his party would cooperate with all the left political parties in their 'united move against the king's "regressive step" '.

March 11
–   The government has given up its efforts to forge an all-party consensus on the code of conduct for peace process and is set to finalise it without consulting the parties,

said Ramesh Nath Pandey, government spokesperson and Minister for Information and Communication.

March 12

– Showing flexible gestures the NC and the UML have given two options to the king, leaving the monarchy to either restore the House of Representatives or form all-party government in consultation with the parties represented in the dissolved lower house.

March 13

– Maoists showed commitment to nationalism and peace by signing a 22-point code of conduct with the government. Maoist negotiation team leader Dr Baburam Bhattarai and the government negotiator Narayan Singh Pun signed the code of conduct in an undisclosed location, and the latter read it out in a press conference. Maoist leader Krishna Bahadur Mahara, a member of Maoists' negotiation team, joined the press meet.

March 16

– Prime Minister Lokendra Bahadur Chand today said that although political parties have demanded the restoration of the House of Representatives, there was no provision in the Constitution which could justify the same.

March 19

– Krishna Bahadur Mahara, an influential leader of CPN Maoist today for the first time made public that his party's economic policy is none other than free market economy.

March 20
- Their Majesties King Gyanendra and Queen Komal left for New Delhi, India on a 10-day long pilgrimage tour. This is His Majesty's second visit to India in nine months after his accession to the throne.

March 21
- Maoist has urged the government to release at least five central level leaders as a precondition for immediate talks. They also want that the government immediately withdraw cases filed against many Maoist leaders including top leaders Prachanda and Dr Baburam Bhattarai at the Patan Appellate Court.
- The All Nepal National independent Students Union-Revolutionary (ANNISU-R), a pro-Maoist student wing, has accused the government of breaching the code of conduct on cease-fire by sending an army and two policemen in civil dress to 'spy' the proceedings of their 'peaceful' programme in Patan Campus in capital.

March 22
- Narayan Singh Pun, the government negotiator for peace talks, said that the peace talk has been delayed as the Maoists have added to their demands one after another.

March 25
- At least 25 Maoists were released from different parts of the kingdom. However, eight others who were re-arrested on Sunday under Public Security Act

immediately after their release by Janakpur Appellate Court were sent to jail.

March 27
– Krishna Bahadur Mahara, member of Maoist peace negotiating team, yet again strongly criticized the government for its 'lack of sincerity' in the peace process.

March 28
– Dr Baburam Bhattarai, the chief co-ordinator of Maoist negotiation team has arrival in capital along with Ram Bahadur Thapa, alias Badal.

March 29
– Maoist dialogue team comes out in open and pledges sincere endeavour for success of peace process.

March 30
– The government conceded what the Maoists have been claiming for long: there are two 'state powers' existing in the country. Narayan Sing Pun said, "There is a balance of power between the government and the Maoists."

March 31
– As Prime Minister Lokendra Bahadur Chand and other political leaders echoed the popular desire for lasting peace in the country today, Maoist leader Dr Babu Ram Bhattarai attacked the Constitution, terming it dead, and exhorting all political forces to come together to build a new Constitution.

– UML and Maoists agreed to form a joint investigation committee to build up friendly relation between the two parties to further facilitate the peace process.

April 1
– In a bid to exchange ideas to bring the present truce to a logical end through all-party agreement, the Maoist negotiators for the peace process, today met separately with Pashupati Shumsher Rana, chairman of Rastriya Prajatantra Party (RPP) and Hridayesh Tripathi, leader of Nepal Sadbhavana Party (NSP)

April 3
– Addressing their first mass meeting at the Tundikhel Open Air Theatre since the start of the 'People's War' seven years ago, leaders of the Maoists, warned the government of serious backlash if present peace process failed.

April 4
– His Majesty King Gyanendra Bir BikramShah Dev has called upon all political parties and civil society to make the peace process a success. His Majesty warned addressing a civic reception held in honour of Their Majesties on behalf of the people in the Far-Western Region that it would be 'against the desire of Nepali people' if any obstacles were created from any quarters.

April 7
– Dr Baburam Bhattarai, coordinator of the Maoist negotiating team accused the king for stalling the peace

process, even after the two months of cease-fire. He was addressing a Maoist rally in Nepalgunj.

April 8
– Prime Minister Lokendra Bahadur Chand said that the political parties were trying to disseminate wrong information about the king and the government.

April 9
– Students cutting across major cities all over the country today launched a string of angry demonstrations, in protest against the killing of Devi Ram Poudel, a student who succumbed to police bullets, during a demonstration against the petro price hike, in Butwal.
– The US Embassy is considering Maoists' request for an appointment with the US officials, US Ambassador in Kathmandu Michael E. Malinowski said, "We are considering the request; we haven't accepted it and we have not rejected it." The US has made it clear that the Maoists first need to establish their seriousness for a credible dialogue, he said.
– Leaders of NC, CPN–UML, PFN and NWPP announced that they are going to launch a protest programme in mid-April. This protest, they claimed would be different from the 1990 movement.

April 12
– Prime Minister Lokendra Bahadur Chand issued a veiled threat to the political parties that they would not be included in the peace process with Maoists if they

don't participate in the all-party meeting scheduled for 13 April.

April 13
- Prime Minister Lokendra Bahadur Chand has proposed forming a high level 'direction committee' comprising of leaders of political parties, to direct the government's negotiating team during talks with the Maoist rebels but the meeting, boycotted by the major political parties.
- Maoist and Government held the first dialogue termed 'goodwill talk' in the capital.
- A meeting of eight student organizations decided to launch a set of massive protest programmes including two rounds of Nepal Bandhs (nation-wide shut down programmes).

April 15
- British Ambassador to Nepal, Keith George Bloomfield, stressed that Nepal should adopt the right policies and attitudes to successfully resolve the Maoist insurgency.

April 15
- Maoists have abducted eight people, Kavre.

April 16
- The government constituted a six-member negotiating team under the leadership of Deputy Prime Minister Badri Prasad Mandal to expedite dialogue with the Maoists.

April 17
- Student strikes paralyse normal activites.

- Armed Maoist rebels have taken eight civilians, including three women, into hostage in a remote village in Rukum district in the mid-western Nepal even after the mutual announcement of the cease-fire and a code of conduct.
- The chief government negotiator for peace talks, Badri Prasad Mandal said that the government has not felt it necessary to appoint any facilitator for ongoing peace talks with the Maoists.

April 18
- Students take strike to new level of violence.
- Museum torched, over two dozen injured, several held.

April 20
- Life in the capital came to a stand-still due to the one-day nation-wide bandh (general strike) called by eight student organizations protesting the hike in petroleum product prices and the death of a student in Butwal on 8 April.

April 21
- Maoists, saying that they wouldn't like to sit for only 'introductory talks' rejected the first round of peace talks proposed by government.
- Maoists abduct 25 locals in Taplejung Tanahun. Chairman of the Maoists, Prachanda, made it clear that the stance of the political parties demanding an all party government would not serve any meaningful purpose to end the continuing stalemate.

April 22
- The Royal Nepal Army (RNA) expressed concern over the growing incidents of violation of the code of conduct by the Maoist rebels and claimed that the army or the security forces had not violated any of the codes agreed upon by the government and the Maoists last month.
- Dr Baburam Bhattarai co-ordinator of the Maoist negotiation team said the king should make his stand clear regarding the political agenda and take positive initiative to move ahead with the peace process.

April 23
- Maoist chief negotiator for peace talks Dr Baburam Bhattarai flayed the Royal Nepal Army for making 'anti-talks' statements at its Tuesday press conference.

April 24
- The visiting Chief of Army Staff of India, General Nirmal Chandra Vij said that India was ready to provide all possible assistance that Nepal needs to combat terrorism.

April 25
- Five political parties warned the king that he should desist from any move to undermine the proposed joint movement against the 4 October royal move.
- Nepali Congress president Girija Parsad Koirala said that the joint movement of the parliamentary parties would be mainly targeted against the monarch.

- Nepal and the United States of America signed Anti-terrorism Assistance (ATA) in the capital, according to a statement issued by the American Center here today.

April 27
- The first round of formal government–Maoist peace dialogue was held today with the Maoists presenting their views on political, social and economic transformation in writing and categorically demanding an interim Constitution and leadership of the proposed interim government.

(Presented at Track-II dialogue of Journalists of India and Nepal, held at Naukuchia Tal, Uttaranchal, India, 3–4 May 2003).

Index